Dear Autun
Thank-you
with us."
Keep grinding!

THE
COMMON
WIFE

×oxo
Lindy

GETTING LOST, DANCING NAKED
AND COLLECTING SEASHELLS

LINDY HUGHES

Shongololo Books
Vancouver, Canada
shongololobooks.com

ISBN: 978-0-9813508-1-3 (paperback)
ISBN: 978-0-9813508-2-0 (ebook)

*This story is the truth, as I remember it. All the interactions and
conversations in these pages occurred, but names and identifying details
have been changed. To respect the privacy of those who may not wish to
have their lives so publicly exposed, I have on occasion combined two
or more people into one, or altered the chronological sequence of events.
I have taken extra care to disguise the pilgrims I met along the Way.
Your secrets are safe with me.*

For David

common
adjective

1. ordinary; of ordinary qualities; without special rank
or position.

2. showing a lack of taste and refinement; vulgar.

PRELUDE

West Vancouver

My husband is sleeping, his pillow trapped under one armpit. I place the letter, neatly folded, on my side of the bed and tiptoe away. If you're going to leave your marriage, you might as well do it on your birthday.

Outside, the only spot of sunlight is on the deck next to the terracotta pot, the one with the dead daisies, so that's where I huddle to wait. My husband should see the letter as soon as he wakes up. Will he be sad that I'm leaving him? Or relieved?

I have not been an easy wife, a good wife. Friends and family often express surprise that my husband has not tired of my shenanigans, like my burlesque adventure. While he did eventually find out about Luna Blue, there are other secrets. The too-much-time I spend in graveyards. Satya with the dreadlocks and the camper van. The stuntman from Texas. Adam. Beautiful Adam. And of course, no one knows about the Crazy.

The Crazy snuck in a while back, around the time my nest started emptying. Mostly, it naps during the day, curled up at the base of my spine, allowing me to do the laundry and grocery shopping as usual. It's at night, when everyone is asleep, that it slithers out, all sparkly and feverish. And then it taunts me, in its gravelly whisper, with questions I can't answer. Questions like where is the Big Life I was meant to live? And who, exactly, stole my destiny? This morning, though, instead of going back to snooze when the sun rose, the Crazy stayed. Insistent, it flicked sparks across my vertebrae until I wrote the letter to my husband, telling him I'm leaving.

Happy birthday, dear Lindy-Lou. Happy birthday to you.

I'm not sure how old I was when my mother first told me the story of my name. I was going to be called Lynn, she said. But at one of her prenatal visits, while waiting for the doctor, my mother saw a very naughty child named Lynn. I'm not sure what made Lynn so very naughty. Was she crying? Tearing magazine pages? Eating the flower arrangements? Regardless, my name was changed to Lindy. Right there in the waiting room.

Even though it wasn't a serious name, like Isadora or Geneviève, names that make me salivate with envy, I would have been happy enough with Lindy. But a few weeks before my birth, my mother crossed paths with a toddler having a tantrum in the pharmacy. *Lindy.* God forbid my mother should have public-tantrum-throwing offspring. So, Lindy-Lou I became. I'm not sure how she

decided on this very English Seussian-sounding name,
since she didn't even speak the language.

She and her three brothers were raised on a farm in
South Africa, in a town called Paarl. Nestled under the
cloud of Table Mountain and apartheid, they were a family
of Afrikaners in a country divided not only by colour, but
language too. When my mother met my father, a rugby
player of Welsh descent, she could not speak a word of
English. That did not stop her from marrying him. Shortly
after their wedding, they moved to Durban, a very English
city on South Africa's east coast, where I was born.
Without family or friends, it must have been a tough
adjustment, more so because no one understood her.

Because my mother did not want me to someday find
myself in the same kind of predicament, she decided that
English would be my first language. She succeeded in her
aim, despite her own struggles with the language. I spoke
early and, she says, with an adult vocabulary. At age two, I
regularly corrected her pronunciation. What a joy I must
have been.

This precociousness, combined with the expectations
of 'goodness' that came with my name, resulted in some
pretty fierce, unwavering delusions of greatness: I was
going to change the world. My life would be anything but
ordinary. No picket fences or diapers for me. I would be
too busy spreading my virtue all over the place. So how did
I end up here, in the suburbs of West Vancouver, married
with kids and pets and a mini-van in the driveway, doing
so many unvirtuous things?

Footsteps in the kitchen – thank goodness! I'm not sure
how much longer I could have stayed out here in the cold.

The door opens and my husband fills the frame. He is calm. As usual. Not even a flighty wife can apparently ruffle his feathers.

"What now?" he says, pulling me up from beside the dead flowers. He is a large man, nearly a foot taller than me. My runny nose squishes against his chest as he hugs me. I must be getting snot all over his shirt.

"I don't know what now," I say into the shirt. I must remember to spray it with Tide before washing it.

He leads me into the living room and sits me down on the sofa. "Thank-you for this," he says, the letter in his hand. "I know I haven't been listening to you."

He is always annoyingly rational. Which makes me feel even crazier. In thirty years, I have yet to see him lose his temper.

"I didn't realise how unhappy you've been," he says, missing the point completely. This isn't about my *happiness*. It's about my *destiny!* "I love you," he says. "Even though you're fucked up."

A tear pops out my one eye. The left one. It's the side where guilt lives. I've got nothing against guilt. It's guilt that reminds us not to steal flowers from the cemetery, or other people's husbands. But guilt can be terribly exhausting.

"Maybe you should go for a walk," he suggests. "Think about things. Walk first. Decide later."

I can do that, I suppose. "OK, I'll go for a walk," I say, sliding my still-cold fingers under my thighs. But any old walk won't be good enough. It needs to be a grand walk. Something in keeping with the drama of this birthday.

Ever since reading *The Canterbury Tales* in the ninth grade, I have been intrigued by the idea of being a pilgrim. Of walking, one step at a time, towards God. And forgiveness. A do-over.

"The Camino!" I say, thrilled by my brilliance.

My husband and I had recently watched *The Way* on Netflix, a movie about a group of pilgrims who trekked 750 kilometres across northern Spain. People have been walking the Camino for more than a thousand years, paying their respects at the shrine of Saint James in the cathedral of Santiago de Compostela.

"The Camino?" my husband says. "That's a long walk." The expression on his face tells me this is not exactly the kind of walk he had in mind.

"Who will go with you?"

"No one. I have to go alone."

"What if you get lost?"

"Don't you remember the movie?" I remind him. "There were signs." I vaguely recall the little yellow scallop shells dotting the road, pointing pilgrims in the right direction.

"But what if something happens to you?"

"It's a pilgrimage. Pilgrims have walked alone for centuries," I say, more confidently than I suddenly feel.

"Yes, and bad guys have been lying in wait to take advantage of stupid pilgrims for just as long."

"It's not like that now," I counter, though really, I have no idea what it's like.

I grab my laptop to do some research while my husband makes breakfast. "This forum says it takes about three weeks to walk the Camino."

He opens his mouth as if to say something, then closes it again. Bacon splatters all over his shirt. More Tide.

"Three weeks is fine," he says.

I am so excited about the destiny waiting for me in Spain, that it completely slips my mind that I don't like walking.

CAMINO DEL NORTE

six months later

Suppose you scrub your ethical skin until it shines,
But inside there is no music.
Then what?
~Kabir

1

Somewhere in Portugalete a clock strikes and the doors to the information centre open. The smile that greets me is framed by a square jaw and shiny black ringlets. A gold badge on his chest says *Matias*, in dainty italics. His eyes are the colour of chocolate lava cake and they glow in the morning light.

"You look like an angel." The words gush from my mouth. *Goddammit!* Having no filter is so inconvenient. Thankfully, this liquid-eyed boy doesn't seem in the least bit offended. He must be used to middle-aged women-in-spandex swooning over him.

"Gracias," he says, his teeth the same shade of white as his shirt. A dimple in his left cheek distracts me, and I briefly forget why I'm here in this converted railway station on the banks of the Nervión River.

Matias tells me, in perfect English, with a sexy Spanish accent, the story of the Vizcaya Bridge, which he gestures toward through the windows. The first transporter bridge in the world, he explains, it's one of very few still working, and it is how passengers have been ferried across the river for more than a hundred years. He seems terribly proud of this, as if he built it with his own two, naked hands.

Mistaking my smitten silence for interest in the bridge, he guides me to the framed sketches on the walls. They show, in excruciating detail, the dimensions of the suspended gondola, and how it can carry two hundred people, six cars and six motorcycles.

I could stand here all day, basking in his beauty, but I have a pilgrimage to get to. Interrupting his story, I tell Matias that I'm doing the Camino, and I'm lost. He looks me up and down, lifting one eyebrow as if he knows something I don't, but should.

"How long will you walk?" he asks.

"Three weeks, I think." Why do I feel chastised by this boy who is probably no older than my son?

His pretty mouth makes a funny whistling noise. Then he tugs on one of Petunia's straps. I've loved Petunia since I first saw her at Mountain Equipment Co-op. She fits me perfectly. No pinching, no squeezing, she feels like a comrade, not a backpack. Maybe he thinks she's too purple for a pilgrimage.

I contemplate unzipping her to show Matias that though she is little, she carries everything I will need on my pilgrimage. But exposing Matias to my underwear would probably be cause for further judgement, so I keep Petunia tightly zipped.

"Do you have a map of the Camino I could see, please?" I ask politely. I am, after all, Canadian.

His eyebrows do that lifting thing again, and he goes behind his counter to get a map. He flattens it on the countertop, uncaps a fat red marker and makes a very large X.

"You are here," he says sharply.

I don't think I like Matias anymore.

He draws a line from the big red X to a spot that seems very far away. "Walk up this hill. At the top you will see the sign to Pobeña. That is the Camino."

I can see what's going through his head. That I'm a silly old lady who didn't even bring a guidebook. I want to defend myself, to tell Matias that everyday practicalities, like maps, seem trivial considering my reason for becoming a pilgrim: to find my Big Life, the one I lost in the suburbs. Instead, I say "Gracias," and leave the building.

Gazing directly into the sunshine, I inhale the same air that pilgrims through the ages have breathed. The Camino de Santiago de Compostela is named after Saint James – Santiago – son of Zebedee and Salome. James and his brother, John, were fishing one day, so the story goes, when Jesus invited them to follow him. They agreed, becoming two of the first apostles. James preached throughout Palestine before traveling to Spain and continuing with Jesus' work in Galicia. When he returned to Jerusalem, he was arrested and beheaded in AD 44, by King Herod, becoming the first apostle to be martyred.

Some say that James' disciples took his body by sea to Galicia. Others, that it was angels who laid him in a rudderless boat. Either way, his relics were forgotten until they were discovered in AD 814 when a hermit named Pelagius saw strange lights in the night sky. Pelagius followed the lights to a small shrine in the remote Galician forest. He reported his findings to Bishop Theodomirus of Iria, who, after three days of fasting, visited the site, along with many of his faithful. He deemed the dancing lights a miracle and when he saw the forested shrine, he decreed that the remains were, indeed, those of James the Great.

Galicia was, at the time, part of the kingdom of Asturias, and when news reached its king, Alfonso II, he ordered a chapel to be built on the site. Once it became common knowledge that the remains of an apostle lay in Galicia, pilgrims started traveling to the tomb. And when the Pope declared that a pilgrimage to Saint James would halve any time spent in Purgatory, the popularity of the Camino, understandably, intensified.

As I turn the corner, my eyes rest on something serpentine slithering out of town. I have never seen anything like this. If a shopping mall escalator and an airport's moving walkway were to procreate, this would be their offspring. But it's outside, in the open air. A steel conveyer belt, it moves slowly up the hill. So dignified, it is quite possibly even more impressive than the transporter bridge behind me. Spaniards are clearly resourceful when it comes to getting around in style.

The only way out of Portugalete is up. It's not that I can't do hills. I've walked from my little home in Eagle Harbour to the Starbucks in Caulfeild Village at least a dozen times. And that's so steep it's practically a mountain. It was the route of my virgin walk a few months ago.

The sales associate at Mountain Equipment Co-op had warned me that I *must* wear in my walking shoes. He told me about his friend whose blisters got so infected on the Camino, that he nearly lost a toe. He was forced to abandon his pilgrimage before reaching Santiago. I was terrified by his gruesome story. So when I got home, I laced up my brand new, bright orange Salomons and set off for Starbucks.

Halfway up Westport Road, a car slowed beside me. It was Carol, one of my neighbours. "Did your car break down?" She sounded panicked. "Can I give you a ride?"

"No thanks, I'm good." I tried to smile.

"No, really! Where do you need to go? I can take you."
She looked ready to burst into tears.

Good Lord! Was I so pathetic that people thought I couldn't walk up a hill for fun? Knowing she wouldn't leave me in peace without an acceptable answer, I said: "I'm practicing leaving my husband."

She brightened immediately. "Oh, okay! See you then," and accelerated up the hill.

And I made it to Starbucks just fine, thank-you very much. I suppose Carol's concern was legitimate. My friends knew I never walked anywhere. Ever. But just because I didn't *like* walking, didn't mean I *couldn't* walk, did it?

The remarkable Spanish walkway up ahead runs next to a perpendicular footpath leading out of Portugalete, giving me a choice, creating the most terrible knot of conflict in my neck. My legs are urging me to step right onto the walkway and ascend gracefully through the early-morning streets. But the annoying glob of conscience on my left shoulder is pulling me the other way, trying to guilt me into using the muscles God gave me. To *walk*. What is Camino etiquette? Can pilgrims *do* transit? Is that cheating?

This is the serpent in the Garden of Eden, tempting me with his promise of an easy ride. I decide to let higher powers decide. This is a pilgrimage after all. I'll close my eyes and spin a few times. When I open them again, the direction I'm facing will tell me which option to take: left and I'll have to walk, right and it'll be permission from above to take the motorised option.

I inhale deeply, close my eyes and start turning slowly. Raising my chin, sun on my forehead, my arms stretch wide, and I spin faster and faster. It's always such a relief to relinquish the responsibility of decision-making. Expelling the last bit of breath, my eyes squint open. I am facing right. *Thank-you, Saint James!*

The walkway raises me up and as I pass my first Camino church, bells start ringing. The bell tower is dirty. Cracked. Falling apart. As if, at any moment, it could come crashing down, and disintegrate into an unholy mess, never to be reconstructed. I know how it feels: the falling apart, the cracks, even the dirty. And I have been sensing my complete and irredeemable destruction for a long time.

The bells get fainter as I leave Portugalete behind. At the top of the hill, the walkway spits me into the countryside. A sign tells me Pobeña is fifteen kilometres away. That's where I hope to sleep tonight, so I set off in the direction of the little yellow arrow.

The fields are filled with goats with enormous horns rolled up on the sides of their heads, like monster cinnamon buns. Black and white cows graze peacefully beside them. There are no people around, so I moo. The cows glance at me, briefly interested. Then they get back to grazing. All except the one nearest me. She stops chewing and tilts her head. Her one eye looks straight into my own eyes. But her other eye seems to be scanning my body, as if she's seeing me onstage in G-string and stilettos. It's the same accusatory look my husband gave me the day he discovered what I'd been doing while he was home alone watching football on TV. Disbelief. Disapproval. Disappointment.

I don't want to be reminded of that day right now, so I turn abruptly, leaving behind the sanctimonious cow, almost tripping over a ginger kitten sleeping in the grass. That's when I notice the cats. So many of them! They run through the fields, chasing butterflies. Or lie curled up at fence posts. They peek at me from behind rocks, then follow alongside, playing with the tall grasses. I feel like a crazy cat lady. It's comforting though. Usually I just feel crazy.

Two kittens run between my legs. One is tabby. The other is black with a white heart shape on its chest. The tabby reminds me of Charlie, my first cat. He was my birthday present soon after I became a big sister and was the reason I brushed my teeth so often. He would jump onto my back as I leaned over the sink, nuzzling my neck, purring. I regularly dressed him in dolls' clothes and pushed him around in the stroller. He would lie exactly as I placed him, on his back, his front paws peeking out over the blanket. He never tried to escape and seemed quite happy to wear a bonnet. Or not. He was a very agreeable cat.

A flash of movement in the distance interrupts my preoccupation with the cats. Still far away, it looks like a horse. Dread settles in my stomach.

I was twelve when my father arranged for us to go riding: himself, my mother, my seven-year-old sister and me. Having no experience with horses, I was given a gentle, well-behaved mare. Fear pitter-pattered in my throat as she approached. I swallowed it quickly, like cough mixture, and mounted her. I could do this.

And then we were off. Not too fast, thankfully. I heaved a little sigh. This was not going to be fun but perhaps I could get through it in one piece.

I tried whispering to my mild-mannered mare, but she must have found my attempts at small talk annoying, and that's when things fell apart. She decided it was time for a gallop. Squeezing my legs tightly against her body, I clutched onto the saddle as the air rushed by. This was not going to end well.

There were trees. Lots of them. Approaching very fast. I was going to be decapitated. My parents would never find my head in this forest. What happened next confused everyone, no one more so than me.

Instead of leaning forward and hanging onto the horse's neck, I leaned backwards. Backwards! Like a circus performer! Which part of my brain could possibly have thought that leaning back was the right thing to do? And where were my arms? Bouncing up and down, limp spaghetti against the horse's back, I closed my eyes. Because if I couldn't see it coming, maybe it wouldn't happen. Because that's how it works, right?

I don't remember how it ended. Did the horse slow down? Did I fall off? Obviously, I didn't die. No bones were broken. And it probably didn't last nearly as long as it felt at the time.

Years later, when I asked my mother about it, she wasn't as traumatised by the event as I would have hoped.

"I don't know why you didn't just follow the rules," she said helpfully. "They told you what to do. You should just have listened."

This was not the first or the last time that I would fail to follow the rules. And always it would come as a surprise. I don't honestly know of anyone who tried harder than me to obey them. To do the right thing. My little sister didn't give a damn about rules. But she was beautiful. Beautiful people are expected to break rules. I wasn't beautiful. I was good. Rules were my lifeline. So how have I ended up breaking so many of them?

It's hard to tell exactly how far away the horse is because the road to Pobeña keeps winding back on itself as I walk through the Spanish hillside. He disappears behind trees and then reappears, his mane streaming behind him as he gallops through the hills. I am mesmerised. And surprised. Instead of fear, I am feeling his joy. And freedom. For nearly twenty-five years I have been bound by marriage and motherhood. But today, here on the Camino, I am untethered. No commitments. No obligations. No stuff.

Everything I will need for the next three weeks is on my back. Petunia weighs in at under five kilograms, because she doesn't carry much: orange flip flops, ugly bucket hat, lightweight sleeping bag, pink silk pillowcase, underwear for five days, two T-shirts, two pairs of socks, leggings and shorts, shampoo, teeny-tiny camping towel, sunscreen, toothbrush and paste, polka dot rain poncho, thin sweater, little purple dress, eight safety pins, a box of princess Band-Aids and mascara, just in case.

In Petunia's left front pocket is my passport. Tucked into it are three letters. One is twenty-four years old and contains only love. The second letter, with its yellow rose, is filled with shame. And the last one was left in my Eagle Harbour mailbox one night. I think of it as the driveway letter and it is part of the Crazy.

In the pocket on the right are two little rocks, one black and one white. Saint and sinner. God will tell me where to leave them on the Way. Because that's what happens on a pilgrimage.

Deep in thought, I come face to face with my nemesis. Standing just a few feet from me, a small wooden fence between us, a rope drags behind him. He's escaped! That explains the disheveled mane. The exhilaration. Unexpected freedom is spectacular. But here's the thing: he's no longer running. He's absolutely still. His coat is shiny. Velvet.

I move closer. One baby step.

He lifts his head, stares me in the eye.

And I am not afraid. It's as if we are asking the same question: what *now?*

2

As the ocean approaches, the cats disappear, one by one, as if by magic. For the past fifteen kilometres, I have been accompanied by butterflies, cows, crazy-horned goats and cats. But all that's ahead of me now is the sea, wild and grey, like the renegade stallion I left behind an hour ago.

One lone kitten remains. He runs in front of me, forcing me to stop. I sit on the steps leading to the beach and he rubs his patchwork body against my shins before hopping onto my lap. He kneads my leggings, his bony back visible beneath his raggedy fur. It's a comforting feeling, those little stabs of pain as his claws connect with my skin through the fabric. His purrs are loud, louder even than the crashing waves.

As a child, I thought that when cats purred it meant that they were happy. The equivalent of a human smile. But in high school biology I learned that purring isn't always a sign of happiness. Sometimes it indicates pain or distress. Purring is apparently an emotional response and some cats even do it while giving birth and that's mostly not a fun endeavour. My childhood cat, Charlie, purred a lot, in and out of the stroller. And I wondered, on that day in biology class, whether I had mistaken some of his purrs for contentment, when he was in fact trying to tell me something else.

I was eight when I found Charlie in the garden one morning. He was stiff and his eyes were open. Some kind of liquid had dribbled out of one side of his mouth. Charlie was dead, poisoned by a neighbour. Just like that he was gone, and I wondered what the point had been of loving him so hard. I don't recall ever playing with the stroller after that.

The skinny Camino cat has had enough of me. He jumps off my legs and disappears up the steps, leaving me to make my way to the beach, cat-less for the first time since Portugalete.

The sand is powder white. I remove my shoes and socks to air my feet, ever-vigilant against blisters.

"Hola!" I hear from behind and two backpackers join me, the first people I've seen since leaving Matias in Portugalete this morning.

We introduce ourselves as I squint into the sun, trying to calculate the height difference between them. Nico is enormous, six-and-a-half feet at least, with hands as big as dinner plates and a most impressive beard. Sylvia is probably three inches shorter than my own five feet, five inches. In one hand she carries a fat dog-eared book. *Camino de Santiago de Compostela* it says, reminding me of how unprepared I am for this pilgrimage.

"You sleeping in Pobeña tonight?" Nico asks me.

"I think so," I say, admitting that I didn't bring a guidebook, so I'm figuring things out as I go.

"That's why I'm with Sylvia," he laughs, startling me with a high-pitched giggle. It's completely endearing and I would squeeze his cheeks if I could find them. "I don't have one either. Sylvia saved me from getting lost a week ago, and we've been walking together since. Why don't you join us?"

I set off with the two of them, ignoring the little voice telling me that I should be walking on my own.

It takes us only a few minutes to reach the albergue – the pilgrim hostel. Payment is by donation. This is possible, in part, because pilgrim accommodations along the Way are run by volunteers – hospitaleros. My donation of €10 gets me a bed for the night, as well as a credencial, my pilgrim passport, which will be stamped and dated at each stop I make along the Camino. The credencial identifies me as a pilgrim – not a common tourist – thus giving me access to the albergues. When I get to Santiago, its stamped pages will be proof of my pilgrimage, entitling me to receive the Compostela, the certificate declaring to all the world that I have completed, on foot, the Camino.

The hospitalero checks my Canadian passport before printing my name on the first page of my credencial: *Lindy-Lou*. It's been years since I've called myself Lindy-Lou. As an adult, I grew tired of explaining my name to people I met, spelling it out loud, telling its story. So Lindy I became. Just Lindy, my mother's greatest fear, the tantrum-throwing child who behaved inappropriately in public.

There are forty beds in the room – twenty bunks. I'm on the bottom against the back wall in the far corner. Nico is above me. If these beds are in any way faulty or weak, I will be dead by morning. Sylvia is in the bunk next to us.

After showering, we head to the restaurant. My first pilgrim meal! On the Camino, I discover, these are inexpensive three-course dinners that include wine. I don't drink alcohol. Well, I do every now and then, but I behave very badly very quickly, so I try not do it in front of strangers. Or God. Nico is more than happy to take on my portion.

During dinner Nico tells me that he is a carpenter. He has lived in the same small town in Switzerland his entire life. Thirty years old, he has been dating his high school sweetheart for fifteen years. But he's known her since toddlerhood. Their parents are lifelong friends.

Sylvia is Italian and the same age as my daughter – twenty-one. She is a nurse in Venice. Quiet, she is content to let Nico do most of the talking. I imagine she is exceptional at her job, gentle and calming, a good listener. Her patients must adore her.

Dessert is ice-cream, thick and fruity. My eyelids grow heavy. We wander back to the hostel and by 9:45 forty adults are all in bed. What is strange is that it *doesn't* feel at all strange. At 10 o'clock the lights are dimmed by an invisible hand. I find Petunia in the darkness, on the little wooden chair next to my bed.

"Good night, Petunia," I whisper.

An unfamiliar peace settles in my chest. It is, I think, gratitude, for the luxury of this time away from life. No cooking, laundry, bill paying, grocery shopping. How lucky am I to be able to disappear from the world and my obligations? To be a pilgrim.

My body softens into sleep.

Bam! Like a bullet between the eyes, the first horrendous reverberation cuts through the silence. And then the rest. A symphony of snorers. I creep deep into my sleeping bag, covering my ears with my silk pillowcase.

God help me.

The horror of nighttime is replaced by a different kind of hell in the morning: forty pilgrims waking up at the same time, all needing the bathroom. Day two is just starting and already I'm doubting my pilgrim-ing ability. I have a hard time peeing when there's a lineup. But somehow, my bladder overcomes its shyness. Exceptionally proud of myself, I swing Petunia over my shoulder and step into the cool air. Nico and Sylvia are in the garden, Sylvia's finger tracing today's route in her guidebook.

"It's twenty-four kilometres to Castro Urdiales," she says.

Nico tightens the straps on his backpack. "You want to walk with us?"

I need to walk on my own. But being alone with my thoughts is so stressful. And I have no sense of direction.

"I'd love to!" I say.

The road out of Pobeña is narrow and steep. We walk in single file. Sylvia leads the way. Nico follows. I am the caboose. When we reach the top, the ocean extends in every direction below us and the sun is beginning to rise.

"You go ahead," I tell them. "I'll catch up." The sun looks like a giant spacecraft rising from the sea. It shoots sparks across the calm waters, as if communicating some kind of intergalactic message. Samantha would love this.

Samantha was my best friend growing up, and we were eight when we saw a UFO. It was soon after Charlie died and we were lying on the furry brown carpet in her dining room, watching the clouds upside down through the window. Samantha didn't have a pet, but she knew how sad I was about Charlie. And she understood that sometimes words don't help. That just lying in the sadness with someone, saying nothing, is the best kind of friendship there is. And so that's what we were doing when we noticed the bright object shimmering in the sky.

"What *is* that?" Samantha sat up.

"I don't know." I sat up too.

"It's not moving."

We moved closer to the window.

"How can it just be hanging there?" I asked. "Planes and things have to move or they fall out of the sky, don't they?"

We were stumped into silence, until Samantha could no longer take it. "Mom!"

Our mothers appeared from the living room. "What *now*?" they said, together.

"What's that thing in the sky?"

Aunty Bettie got her binoculars from the kitchen. "I think it's a UFO," she said, peering through the little lenses. Aunty Bettie wasn't actually my aunt. We called all the adults we knew *aunty* or *uncle*.

"A UFO? That's just rubbish," said my no-nonsense mother. "Turn on the radio."

As we passed the binoculars between us, listeners, hundreds of them, called in to the radio station to report an unidentified flying object in the skies above us. Samantha and I were too excited to speak.

But why was my mother taking so long with the binoculars? And why was she staring across the road instead of up in the sky? Had the UFO moved? I was about to ask for the binoculars when she thrust them Aunty Bettie's way.

"Ken's car! In Barbara's driveway," she sputtered.

"No!" gasped Aunty Bettie. "In the middle of the day? While Doris is stuck at home with the kids?"

"Shame. Poor Doris," my mother sighed. "And she's such a *good* person."

"Yes, it's not her fault she's so dowdy, at home all day on her own with three small children."

Samantha and I didn't know Uncle Ken or Aunty Doris, but I felt sorry for Aunty Doris. I hoped her three children appreciated her staying home, being dowdy for them, whatever dowdy was.

"That tart, Barbara!" Aunty Bettie exploded, binoculars still glued to her face. "I never liked her, with her tight shirts and mini-skirts."

"She's always had her eye on Ken," my mother added in such a thin voice that I had to strain to hear it.

Usually when our mothers talked about grown-up stuff in front of us, they used a frustrating kind of code that we couldn't understand. But that day was different. In passing the binoculars back and forth, they seemed to forget that we were there.

Samantha and I were confused. The only tarts we knew were the kind you ate. And how did you put your eye on someone? Maybe there was something wrong with Aunty Barbara's eye. Maybe that's why Uncle Ken was parked in her driveway in the middle of the day while Aunty Doris was home caring for the children. But we couldn't interrupt our mothers to suggest this. We were too busy being invisible.

"How long do you think it's been going on?" asked my mother.

"Who knows? Could be years, with the two of them working together," said Aunty Bettie. "*Very* convenient."

I knew Samantha was thinking the same thing as me: if they worked together, maybe they were doing homework now. Even though we were only in the third grade, Samantha and I sometimes had group projects we had to work on together after school. Or maybe Aunty Barbara had left her sweater at work, and Uncle Ken was returning it to her. I forgot my sweater at school at least once a week.

"And that brassy hair. So common." More new words.

We learned so much that day, Samantha and me. But after a while of watching our mothers snuggled up close to one another at the window, we snuck outside. In the back garden, we watched the silver blob above us.

Why were our mothers so angry with Aunty Barbara when it was Uncle Ken who had driven away from his wife and children, and parked in Aunty Barbara's driveway? Being an adult was so confusing, specially a lady adult. It didn't sound like much fun, with people spying on you, to see if you were breaking the rules.

Maybe Aunty Barbara didn't know about the too-short-skirt and too-tight-shirt rule. Like the time in first grade when I coloured the tree trunks purple and Sister Patricia told me they had to be brown. Until that day, I hadn't known that there were rules for the colours in the crayon box. What if I broke a lady rule someday that I didn't know about, and another lady's husband came into my driveway in the middle of the day, and the people who knew the rules whispered about me from behind their shiny windows and their binoculars?

"What's dowdy?" Samantha asked.

"I don't know."

"We have to find out," she said, her eyes growing wide. "Because what if my husband parks his car in another lady's driveway one day because I'm dowdy? That would make me very sad."

While Samantha's fear was of dowdiness, mine was of tartiness. As it turns out, our mothers had it all wrong. I successfully escaped tarty for the next forty years, living dangerously close to dowdy. But it would not stop another lady's husband from walking into my driveway one day. And his words, as he leaned into my tie-dye T-shirt, would make me question the meaning of everything I'd ever believed to be true. And right. Not to mention the impact they would have on the Crazy hibernating in my spine.

3

The sun rises quickly and I catch up with Nico and Sylvia at the entrance to a tunnel cutting through the mountain. It's just about the right size for the seven dwarves, and I quell the urge to sing *heigh-ho, heigh-ho, it's off to work we go!* This is not home. These are not my people. I need them to think I'm sane, for just a little while longer at least.

Once through the tunnel, the path winds between long grasses. The trees are sparse. Their branches and leaves poke out on one side, as though a ferocious wind is at work, even though there is not a whiff of a breeze this morning. We have seen no one else since leaving the albergue, which is bizarre considering how many of us woke up at the same time.

We leave the cliffs behind and clouds rush in as we walk down towards a valley. The road descends steeply into a village and we find a tiny café just as the rain comes down.

Nico orders café con leche. I follow suit. Never before have I tasted anything this delicious. Maybe it's because we've been walking for three hours. I order a second cup.

Then a third. Caffeine alone will get me to our next stop, wherever that is.

When we can no longer delay, we prepare for the rain outside. Sylvia and Nico have navy blue rain jackets and waterproof covers for their packs. I have a plastic poncho with multi-coloured polka dots.

"Nice dots," Nico giggles.

What was I thinking when I bought this? Petunia and I must look like a giant popsicle. As usual, I got it on a whim, without weighing up the pros and cons. Coping with the consequences afterwards. Like so many of my decisions in the past few years. At least the worst outcome in this case is Nico's laughter. Unlike the aftermath of some of my other choices. Like Luna Blue. And Adam.

The drizzle follows us all the way to Castro Urdiales, the seaside village where we are spending the night. The beige albergue overlooks a bullfighting arena. I deposit Petunia on my bed and walk across to the arena, where I come face-to-face with something I haven't seen in a very long time. My father's sword!

I was six-and-a-half when my father went to Europe on business, bringing back with him a sword from Spain. Taller than me, it was nestled in an elaborate silver sheath. Red velvet peeked out between the sheath's metal curls. With his hand over mine, my father and I pulled the weapon from its casing. Sparks of light shot in every direction, blinding me with fervour. I pictured myself galloping across the face of the earth on a white stallion, sword held high in victory, flames of righteousness in my wake. Saviour of the Universe! (That was before I realised I had horse issues.)

The sword on the poster here, on the arena wall, is almost identical to my father's. I lean in to examine it, trying not to touch the yellowed paper or the grubby wall. It seems to be advertising some kind of bullfighting and

worship event. Surely not? I can't make sense of the poster
— a sword, a bull and Jesus floating on a cross — so I walk
back to the albergue.

A black-haired boy is sitting on the steps. "You like
bullfighting?" he asks me.

"I don't know," I say. "I've never seen a bullfight. Isn't
it quite violent?"

He shrugs, as if violence is to be expected, and tells me
that he comes from a long line of bullfighters.

"Are you a bullfighter then?"

"Oh no," he smiles. "I will be becoming a doctor."

"Have you always wanted to be a doctor?"

"Since when I stopped wanting to be a magician." His
speech is coloured by all sorts of lilts and rhythms.

"A magician?" I sit next to him on the steps. "Like
Harry Potter?"

"No, like Merlin," he says.

"What's the difference?"

He looks at me as if I'm stark raving mad. "Harry Potter
is not a real person."

Oh, of course. And Merlin is. I like this boy.

"And you? What is the first thing you wanted to be?"
His words twirl between us.

"A ballerina."

When I was six, I begged my mother to sign me up for
ballet class. She thought it was a phase that I would
outgrow and made me wait. A whole year. My first lesson
in delayed gratification, a concept I would go on to
embrace wholeheartedly. Catholic school encouraged that
sort of thing.

Ballet class took place in the church hall. There was a solitary mirror next to the shiny black piano, angled so that the pianist could see the dancers. I inhaled the dust particles and my insides smiled. *This* was my place. It didn't matter who I was outside these walls, how many times I accidentally coloured outside the lines or in an inappropriate shade. In this hall it was me and the music and God himself, swirling in the sunshine splintering through the windows high above.

Madame wore a wraparound skirt fastened in a bow on her very upright ballerina back. When she pointed her toes, in her pale pink pumps, her foot arched into a perfect rainbow shape. I prayed to have feet like hers someday and I worked very hard, desperate for any small words of praise. They were hard to earn and obliterated in an instant by poor posture or sloppy toes. Laziness was second only to flat feet in the ballet book of sins.

God ensured that my dedication, and very long wait, was rewarded. I was chosen to be the L in LOVE for the year-end ballet recital. I wore a pink satin tutu with a heart on the front. The heart was made of velvet – the same colour as the velvet that protected my father's sword. Inside the heart was the letter L, for Love. For Lindy-Lou. I adored that tutu. I'm pretty sure I was the only seven-year old with fully-formed calf muscles, and I was built more like a wrestler than a dancer. But in that tutu, I was a fairy princess.

We performed our recital at the Opera House! The stage curtains were an other-worldly combination of crimson and purple, a shimmering waterfall dividing us magical beings onstage from the ordinary folk out in the audience. The real world was filled with confusing rules and expectations. But in this kingdom of tights and tulle there was no right or wrong. There was only the story, and the telling of it with your body and music.

I watched from the wings as the curtains rose in their elegant folds of velvet, disappearing into the abyss above me. And then it was time to dance. I had expected to see the audience, but they remained hidden in the darkness. I felt them, though, in pulses of energy. Like love.

Forty years later, a lifetime really, performing a completely different kind of dance on an altogether otherwise kind of stage, the Crazy spiraling through my veins, I would feel it again: the magic of stepping out of the shadows, exposing myself to strangers and being transformed by their applause.

"A ballerina," says the boy who would be Merlin. "A ballerina is very much like a magician. She must be making a world where people are believing that everything is beautiful and forever. You would be a good ballerina, I think. There is magic in your eyes."

Nico and Sylvia join us on the steps, so I don't have to respond. Don't have to tell this boy that magic in the eyes is, sadly, not enough. Not for ballet. Not for anything.

My silence goes unnoticed and I slip away to sleep, earlier than the others, and dream of pudgy ballerinas, bulls in red velvet and dead babies.

Babies first appeared in my dreamlife in my early twenties. Over the years, I have dropped babies from balconies or into the ocean. In my sleep, I have packed babies in suitcases, forgotten to feed them, or fed them so much that they exploded. Babies have slipped from my arms, cracking their heads on tables with very sharp corners. You do not want to be a baby in my dreams.

I'm relieved when morning comes. I get ready quickly and wait outside for Nico and Sylvia, eager to escape last night's dreams.

Once we leave the albergue and the crumbling arena behind, I feel lighter. The town of Castro Urdiales ends abruptly and we're on clifftops again. We hear the bells before we see the sheep. Brown faces with shaggy blonde hair, they ignore us as they munch away at the grass. We try to squeeze between them but we're surrounded. Stuck.

"My father used to tell us stories about sheep like this, all warm and fuzzy and friendly," Nico says. "But they were really wolves in disguise, waiting to trick children into playing with them, before gobbling them up."

"How old were you?" Sylvia is horrified.

"Five? Maybe six? My brother and sister were even younger," he giggles. "My dad was the most awesome story-teller." He doesn't give Sylvia or I time to interrupt. "He'd switch the bad guys and the good guys all the time. We'd never know who was going to be the villain."

"What do you mean?" Sylvia asks. I suspect she believes that good is good and bad, bad. Simple. Polar opposites. Easy to identify. I believed that too when I was twenty-one.

"One night Little Red Riding Hood would be a sweet little girl picking flowers to cheer up her granny," Nico explains. "And the next she'd be making a flower potion to drug granny so she could steal the cash in her money box to buy a new cape."

"Isn't that messed up?" Sylvia says.

"Probably," Nico laughs. "But so much fun."

The sheep are still happily grazing, keeping us trapped in the long grass.

"Do you have a favourite fairy tale?" Nico asks me.

"I always loved the story about the white and the black wolf," I say. "But I'm not sure it's a real fairy tale." One fuzzy-faced sheep glances up briefly, as though concerned by all this talk of wolves.

"Oh, I don't think I know that one," says Sylvia.

Nico doesn't either, so I recite the story about the old man who told his grandson that there are two wolves that live inside each of us. *"They are always battling each other, the white and the black wolf, every minute of the day,* the old man said to the little boy. The boy looked at his grandfather with big eyes and said *which one wins, Grandpa?"* Nico and Sylvia are staring at me with the same big eyes, waiting. I use my old man voice: *"The one you feed, my boy. The one you feed."*

"What an awesome story!" Nico's eyes are sparkling. "I'm going to remember that."

The sheep start moving, freeing us up to be on our merry pilgrim way. So I don't tell Nico and Sylvia that I think Grandpa was misguided. When I first heard the story, I also thought it was beautiful. And I took it to heart, feeding that white wolf until he just about exploded. But what I discovered, much later, in the midst of the Crazy, was that *not* feeding the black wolf doesn't make him go away. It just makes him hungrier.

4

Comparing our favourite fairy tales makes the time pass quickly and before any of us is expecting it, we are on the outskirts of Laredo. Sylvia leads the way to the albergue, a centuries-old convent that looks more like a prison than the home of the nuns of the Trinitarian Order. The wooden door is shut tight and Nico rings the doorbell. A small square in the centre of the door squeaks open, and two eyes peek out from behind steel bars. The tiny nun invites us in, stamps our credenciales and tells us that there will be a special pilgrim blessing this evening in the chapel. I can hardly wait!

We dump our backpacks in our room, and go in search of a grocery store. After walking more than thirty kilometres, it's time for nuts and chocolate. And the beach.

"Laredo is known for La Salvé, one of the longest beaches in northern Spain," Sylvia reads from her guidebook. Laredo's population of 12,648 apparently more than doubles in summer, but right now we are the only people on the beach. It's early June, and the summer tourist season has not yet begun.

"Hey! These are Camino shells!" Nico picks up one of the faded shells scattered around us on the sand. Both he and Sylvia have larger, plastic versions attached to their backpacks. It identifies them as peregrinos – pilgrims. The iconic Camino symbol is painted on sidewalks, walls, trees, even cobblestones and rocks, directing pilgrims to Santiago.

"What's so special about these shells?" I want to know.

Sylvia explains that medieval pilgrims used them as bowls for food and water along the Way. "But they're also a metaphor. You see these lines?" She points to the shell in Nico's palm. "They represent all the different routes to Saint James' tomb. Sometimes you walk *towards* the fat body of the shell." She runs her finger along the longest groove towards the raised centre.

"Only sometimes?" Nico asks.

"Yes, it depends which part of the Camino you're on. In some regions, you walk in the opposite direction, away from the body."

"That seems really confusing," he says, examining the little scallop in his very large hand.

"That's why there are usually arrows too." The picture in her guidebook shows a yellow arrow painted underneath the scallop on a stone wall.

"Why don't you have a shell?" Nico asks me.

I can't tell him that I think it's stupid to put an artificial shell on your backpack. Nor can I confess that I don't want to be the same as everyone else – a common pilgrim. So instead I say, "Maybe I'll find one here."

There are hundreds of whitewashed scallops on the beach, each with the tiniest of holes, as if pricked by a hot needle. I gather a handful, examining them closely. They are perfect. Much lovelier than the plastic ones. I will take some with me and add them to the shell collection that lives in my passage cupboard at home in Vancouver.

When the three of us get back to the convent, streams of pilgrims are leaving the chapel. Mass is over! The priest has left the building. What is *wrong* with me? My first opportunity to receive a Camino blessing and I blow it by prancing about barefoot on the beach like a teenager, stealing Spanish shells. How will I ever find that elusive thing I've been searching for since I was fifteen – the day I persuaded Father Ignatius to listen to my sins?

I had been baptised in the Dutch Reformed Church, because of my mother's Afrikaner roots, and confirmed Methodist simply because that was the church nearest our house.

It was at Sunday school, in the basement of the Methodist Church, that I was introduced to Adam and Eve, Samson and Delilah, Joseph and his technicolour dream coat. And then there was Noah's Ark and Jacob's ladder ascending to Heaven. But it was Moses I most loved. Moses, who escaped death as an infant when his mother set him afloat in the bulrushes. Who led the Israelites out of captivity, wandering in the wilderness for forty years. Moses, to whom God gifted the Ten Commandments, written in stone on Mount Sinai. I was distraught when I realised that Moses never made it into the promised land. After all that.

While Sunday school was all about the stories, Catholic school was serious stuff. It was there that I learned about the sacraments and the doctrines, about Heaven, Hell and Purgatory, the consequences of sin. I was allowed to attend Friday mass at school with everyone else. But I was not allowed to receive communion because I was not Catholic. I like to think that God would be above that kind of pettiness, but this was not a conversation I intended to have with the nuns.

I'm not sure whether the other girls, the bona fide Catholics, believed that the little round wafer the priest popped into their mouths was really the body of Jesus, or that the red wine they sipped from the silver chalice was truly his blood. But this was Father Ignatius' justification for not letting me join communion lineup. The Methodist Church, he told me, believed that communion was merely symbolic, not the real deal. So, while the rest of my classmates headed to the altar to receive Jesus' body and blood, I was forced to stay on my knees in the pews to ponder the inadequacies of my lesser denomination. I used this time wisely by trying to figure out how I could get into confession.

I'd seen movies where the priest waited in a little booth, apparently napping. The transgressor entered through a curtained entrance on one side and opened the little square grille that separated priest from sinner. I wasn't sure whether this was to preserve the confessor's anonymity, or to spare the priest from being sullied by the sin. Probably both. Once all was confessed, a penance imposed and the trespasser forgiven, all would be fine again in the universe of good and evil. Until next time.

This whole process appealed to my love of secrets and rituals. I knew for a fact that it was not only Catholics who sinned, so I pled my case. It took a few meetings with Mother Superior, but eventually I was granted permission to confess. Being not-Catholic, I was banned from the confessional and had to visit the priest in his office instead. That made me a little sad, but it was better than nothing.

At age fifteen, I was a most conscientious rule-follower. I didn't argue with my superiors, never left school property without my hat and blazer, had never been on a date. I didn't wear mascara and I kept my naked fingernails even shorter than regulation length. My days were filled with school, homework, choir practice and ballet, so my confession must have been uncommonly boring. Perhaps it included my envy of my little sister, of the ease with which she sailed through life and her disdain for rules, which made me follow them even more rigidly. While she flitted about all pretty and popular, I was living up to the expectations of Goodness that came with my name.

While I don't remember my confession to Father Ignatius that day, nor what penance he imposed, I will never forget his parting words. "God has a plan for you," he said, the white collar of his priesthood straining slightly. "With time and patience, all will be revealed." I held my breath. "Pray. And listen closely," he whispered.

I closed my eyes. *I knew it!* I *was* special!

Father Ignatius rested his thumb between my eyebrows. "In nomine Patris et Filii et Spiritus Sancti," he said, making the sign of the cross on my forehead with his blessed fingers. *In the name of the Father and of the Son and of the Holy Ghost.*

Every detail after leaving his office is etched in my marrow: the fluffiness of the clouds, the purple bougainvillea collapsing over the brick wall, the air rushing across my thighs as my summer school uniform flew about while I skipped down the stairs and the smile that radiated from my solar plexus. My heart was enormous, expanded by the Holy Spirit. With the blessing I had just received, and the sword of righteousness under my father's side of the bed, I was the Chosen One.

It's this feeling of absolution and purpose that I've been chasing for what feels like a lifetime, and I have just blown my chances by missing mass tonight. Everyone leaving the chapel appears so blessed. So pure. I walk through the darkened convent towards my bunk. And there she is, at the end of the hallway, a green-faced nun with her hands folded piously in her lap. She is staring at me crookedly and I feel the heat of judgement in my thighs. Sister Bernadette.

Sister Bernadette was my tenth grade biology teacher. Through a democratic process of one-girl-one-vote, I had been elected class captain that year, which made me more than a little anxious. From what I understood, the class captain was the spokesperson for the entire class. I took my class captain responsibilities seriously, even though I had no idea what they were. If only there was a *Class Captain Rulebook*. Rules made me feel safe. Maybe if I was Catholic I would have known the rules. But I wasn't Catholic. And yet, here I was, at Catholic school, a class captain with a stupefying fear of displeasing anyone in authority. And Sister Bernadette was authority. More to the point, she was a nun, which meant that her power came from God Himself.

During class one morning, not long after my confession in Father Ignatius' office, Sister Bernadette asked me something I didn't understand. Did it have something to do with my class captain duties? Or was it something personal? Her tone confused me. It sounded like a rhetorical question, but one that she was daring me to answer. It felt like a prelude to disaster. Like the time my thumb disappeared in the bread slicing machine. One minute, everything was fine, neatly sliced bread piling up on the counter. The next, I watched my thumb disappear into the slicer, knowing the outcome would not be good. Sister Bernadette hovering over me felt like the bread slicer all over again.

My chair made a scraping sound as I stood. When someone in authority addressed you, you did not remain seated. Sister Bernadette went fuzzy before my eyes. Holding onto my desk with one hand, tugging at my tie with the other, I tried to breathe. Sister Bernadette repeated her question, still blurry. The silence in the classroom filled my head. The girls in the front row were staring at their desks. No one made eye contact with Sister Bernadette. Or with me. Still not knowing what she wanted me to say, I said nothing. That did not help.

Sister Bernadette's body quivered. Her face grew pink. One strand of her frosty hair had escaped and her voice was thinner than usual. It triggered a fire in my knees that crept slowly up my thighs, my hips, my stomach and then my chest. When the heat reached my neck and cheeks it turned me entirely red. Redder even than Sister Bernadette. I tried to make sense of the words coming out of her mouth, but all I could focus on was my burning body. Only once the flames reached my ears could I hear what she was saying.

"You think you're so perfect," she spat. "Well, you're not. You are *far* from perfect."

The bell rang and Sister Bernadette exited in a storm of white stockings and black shoes. Hands clasped behind her, she moved so quickly that her habit tremored. I was left standing, heat burrowing ferociously into my bones.

Sister Bernadette never mentioned the incident again. And I never had the chance to ask her what it was that I did or did not do that she found so upsetting, so imperfect, so wicked. But here, in the quiet darkness of the convent in Laredo, is my opportunity to dispel some of that white-hot shame.

"Shame on you," I say to the green-faced nun staring at me from the wall. "Shame on you, Sister Bernadette, for abusing your power. Shame on you for leaving me to wonder what it was that I did that was so terribly sinful. Shame on you for making my teenage-self feel like a bad person. Shame. On. You." I walk away, turning my back on her, thirty-six years after she turned hers on me.

5

I'm not a violent person, but I would love to thrust my knife slowly into the throat of the woman next to me. Maybe that would shut her up.

Nico, Sylvia and I are waiting for breakfast at the enormous dining table in Laredo. A group of pilgrims has joined us and one of them is complaining loudly about the lack of greens in Spain. She and her friends are from Arizona and they're cycling the Camino. How does cycling even count? That's like being half a pilgrim at best.

I'm still grumpy about missing the pilgrim blessing last night, and this woman is making things worse. *Really?* I want to say to her. *You're on vacation. You spend your days cycling through some of the most stunning scenery on the planet. When you get thirsty, you stop for a drink. When you get hungry, you stop for a meal. The weather is perfect. The accommodation is not only inexpensive, but comfortable. You're being served a warm breakfast by nuns. But you're moaning because you can't find iceberg lettuce?*

To tune out her whiny voice, I glance away, straight into the glaring eyes of the green-faced nun. Again! Who *is* she?

Slightly askew, on the wall opposite me, she seems to be a Catholic version of the Mona Lisa. I thought I had it out with her in the passage last night, but she is staring no less judgementally at me this morning.

I have always admired people who can swear with abandon. Profanities trickle easily across my sister's tongue. But they get stuck in my throat. I decide to remedy this sad flaw of mine right here, on this Sunday morning in Spain. A pilgrimage is as good a place as any to start cursing. A convent even better.

Fuck you, Sister Bernadette, I think. *I never thought I was perfect, even though I spent my entire life trying to be good.* I breathe in deeply between each imagined word. *Fuck. You. Sister. Bernadette.*

Grabbing a muffin, I excuse myself from the table, leaving behind the whiny cyclist and the green nun. As I step across the convent threshold, I say out loud, "Just fuck, fuck, *fuck* you, Sister Bernadette." *Holy Mary, Mother of God, cursing is so much better than a blessing.*

From the Convent courtyard, Laredo's red roofs are framed by the purple mountains in the distance. It's already warm, but there's a salty freshness in the air that you find only near the ocean.

There are many roads to Santiago. The most popular is the Camino Francés, the French Way. This was the route in the Netflix movie my husband and I had watched. I chose Camino del Norte, the Northern Way because Google had said that it is was more isolated. There would be fewer pilgrims, fewer distractions I reasoned. But already I have failed dismally at walking alone. I will have to remedy this soon. But not yet.

As I finish my muffin, Sylvia is at the door. "We have two options today," she says. "The first is via ferry to Santoña, and then a walk along the beach before heading inland to Güemes."

"What's the other option?" Nico asks.

"On the highway and longer."

"No choice then is there?" says Nico. "Ferry it is." And off we go.

'Ferry' is a much-too-grand name for the rusty little boat waiting for us. Metal seats line the perimeter, with lifebuoys the colour of my shoes attached to the seats. I sit as close as I can to a buoy. Just in case. A laundry line of national flags runs the length of the boat. Neither Canada nor South Africa is represented.

Boats are not my favourite thing. I dream often of drowning. And I get sea-sick. Fortunately, the water is calm and the trip does not last long. I repeat *The Lord's Prayer* in my head until we arrive safely at Santoña. I step onto dry land. *Amen.*

The route veers inland and it gets steamy very quickly. Too hot to talk, the only sound is the crunch of our shoes on gravel. No farmers in the fields, or even livestock. All have taken refuge somewhere cooler. Only pilgrims are stupid enough to be out in this.

The Chapel of San Julian de Güemes appears, like a mirage, out of nowhere. In silence, we file into the darkness. Cool relief. Plastic baby Jesus lies on the altar. At his feet is a bouquet of dried geraniums, the colour of dead skin, interspersed with crocheted off-white roses. No housekeeping has taken place here since the chapel was built many centuries ago. I collapse onto a rickety chair in the shadows and rest my cheek against the cold stone.

Baby Jesus is illuminated by the beam of light squeaking through the church door. And the smell is a familiar one. Ancient wood and dust particles and God. It's the smell of ballet class. As I lean forward to get a better view of the crocheted flower arrangement, my chair creaks. And, in what seems to be a Camino phenomenon, I am transported back through time – to the day I narrowly escaped making a deal with the Devil, when I was just eleven years old.

It was the best of ballet. And the worst. The Concours de Ballet was an annual dance competition, where I feared that someday I would witness a tutu'd ballerina scratching out the eyes of a rival dancer.

My hair was meticulously sprayed in a high bun. I was always surprised at the end of a competition to find my hairline in the same place as before. On one occasion I watched, in the dressing room mirror, as my teacher yanked my hair into a ponytail and coiled it tightly. She anchored the arrangement to my scalp with three-inch hairpins and my eyes changed shape, growing wide, not in surprise or even pain, but out of sheer necessity as my forehead was pulled away from my eye sockets. Ballet is not for the faint-hearted.

Competition days were organised by age group and dance style. I would be performing my classical ballet solo with the other eleven-year-olds after lunch. Waiting in the auditorium, I was watching the tap dancers, intrigued. They made so much noise! In ballet, the only sound allowed, except for the music, was silence. Tapping seemed like fun.

My teacher leaned towards me and whispered, "Look at their ankles." What was I looking for? Sparkles? Frills? Bells?

I peeked at my own ankles, but they were covered with socks. Really ugly socks. In pursuit of a perfect grooming score, our satin slippers were never permitted to touch the surface of anything but the stage floor on the day of the performance. Not a smidgeon of dust could sully them. It was a kind of Seussian wonderland, with hundreds of ballerinas in satin and tulle, elaborate hairdos and hideous socks. Me and my Grinch name, Lindy-Lou Who, fit right in. Thankfully, no one ever tried to scratch out my eyes. It's one of the perks of being not-good-enough. You don't incite envy.

I rolled down one sock. My ankle and the ankles onstage appeared, for all intents and purposes, identical. Except that mine was considerably more confined, with satin ribbons wrapped tightly, painstakingly stitched to prevent escape and then secured with hairspray. The indent at my Achilles could surely not be healthy. The tapper ankles seemed, I suddenly realised, a lot freer.

As I leaned forward to get a better view of their feet, my teacher hissed: "All that ungraceful stomping gives them fat ankles. And those ugly fishnet stockings! So common!"

Now common was a word I knew. I understood that it was the worst possible thing you could be. It's how you ended up with other people's husbands in your driveway in the middle of the day.

And I suddenly felt so lucky to be sitting with this beautifully uncommon teacher of mine. And so thankful that she had saved me from trading in my ballet shoes for the tapping kind, from selling my soul.

Thirty-six years later, her words would come drifting back through space and time as I waited backstage in a drafty East Vancouver theatre. Wearing a scarlet corset, lacy thigh-high stockings and sequin stilettos for my debut performance as Luna Blue, I would glance at my ankles. No fishnets or tap shoes. Not common at all.

From my wonky chair in the shadows, I see Nico and Sylvia leave the church, so I follow.

Dipping my fingers in the brass bowl at the entrance, I pause to make the sign of the cross. *In the name of the Father and of the Son and of the Holy Ghost.* Forehead, heart, shoulder, shoulder. I press my damp fingertips together to finish my prayer. *Amen.*

As I turn to close the door, my ankle twists awkwardly and a white-hot pain shoots up the back of my leg. *Holy crap!* Too late, I apologise for sticking my Protestant fingers into Catholic holy water.

When we arrive in Güemes, I am tired and hot, and my ankle is pounding furiously. While we wait in the long lineup at the albergue, I remove my shoes and socks. My feet are burning up and my right ankle is twice the size of the left. Whatever happened as I left the church earlier, was clearly not good. Fortunately, Nico and Sylvia are too trapped in their own discomfort to notice mine.

With our credenciales stamped at last, a volunteer shows us around. The albergue is huge, with three wings surrounding a communal grassy area. There are pilgrims everywhere: showering, hanging laundry, playing cards, napping in the sun. An enormous map of del Norte is painted along one whitewashed wall. It depicts the route from where it starts in the Pyrenees, all the way to Santiago and then on to Finisterre, once thought to be the western-most point of the world. A black circle marks Güemes, where we are now. Santiago de Compostela is a small dot in the distance.

"Shit," says Nico. "We still have so far to go."

The two of us collapse under a tree. My fat ankle breathes a little sigh of relief. Sharing our shade is a young couple. He's on his back, a towel rolled under his head, reading. She is burrowed into one of his armpits, eyes closed. This is the way my children and I used to snuggle when we read fairy tales. The boy absent-mindedly twirls a strand of the girl's hair, which is the colour of whole wheat bread.

"Where did you meet your husband?" Nico asks me, glancing at the boy as he turns a page of his book, then goes back to twirling his girlfriend's hair, as if that's what his fingers were born to do.

"At a student pub."

"But you don't drink?"

"That night at the pub had something to do with it," I laugh.

"So what was it about him that attracted you?"

"He had a beard." *Oh God. Did I say that out loud?*

"A beard?" Nico tugs at the hair on his face giving me a crooked smile.

"Yes, he looked like Kenny Loggins. But you're too young to know who that is."

"Thirty's not that young," he says. "And who doesn't know *Footloose?* So what happened the night you met?"

"Not much. He remembers the shoes I was wearing. Converse with some kind of writing on them, apparently. I remember his beard. I drank two glasses of red wine and spent the rest of the night vomiting."

"And then?" he persists.

"Marriage wasn't part of my plan. I was going to save the world."

"So, how *did* you end up married?" He is struggling to put the pieces together.

A gong interrupts our conversation, reverberating through the thick evening heat. The pilgrims around us move, en masse, towards a large room on one side of the property. They leave everything behind. Card games. Books. Half-folded laundry. Coffee cups. Like zombies. This is most peculiar. And kind of creepy. There must be at least a hundred people here, and it's the first time I've heard a gong at an albergue. Or seen any kind of mass group behavior. Have we stumbled into a cult? Goosebumps run up my arms and legs.

Jonestown.

The mass murder-suicide at the Peoples Temple Agricultural Project, otherwise known as Jonestown, happened just two days after my fifteenth birthday. At the time, I could not fathom how an apparently ordinary man like Jim Jones enticed more than nine hundred people to drink Kool-Aid laced with poison. Parents murdered their own children – their babies. They watched them die before drinking the cyanide themselves. What did that say about humans? Is our need to belong so desperate that it overpowers all else, dragging us over the edge to commit such atrocities? And did Jim's hold over his people have anything to do with the upright white collar of holiness he wore?

It was Jim Jones who solidified my do-gooding desires. As I watched the events unfold on television, I was certain that I could have changed the trajectory of his life (and saved the hundreds who died that day), simply by loving him unconditionally. By listening to his story. Had he looked into my eyes, I believed then, I would have been able to lead him along the path of righteousness instead of murder.

Now, I suspect I would simply have crumbled under his gaze and done exactly what he commanded. But at fifteen, I knew, with the certainty that only the Chosen possess, that saving the world was what I was born to do. Father Ignatius had said so.

"God, I'm hungry," Nico interrupts my maudlin thoughts. "Let's go. The sooner we get this over with, the sooner we eat." Nico is always hungry. Our €10 donation at Güemes includes dinner and breakfast, but before dinner we're all required to attend a talk. That's what's happening now. At least, I'm hoping that's all this is.

We follow the rest of the pilgrims up the stairs into the large room lined with benches. Sylvia is already there, examining the framed photographs on the walls. There are so many of us that the seats fill quickly, the rest of the crowd sitting on the floor, creating a symphony of different languages. Pilgrims are stuffed into every cranny, their faces transfixed.

Nico's arm, squeezed tightly next to mine, feels like a furnace. My eyelids are sticky with sweat and claustrophobia. There are too many people in the room. And not enough air. Why are there no open windows? *Think about something else.*

I focus on the painted dot on the wall outside, representing Santiago de Compostela, which I can just see from where I'm sitting. It reminds me of the pale blue dot, a photograph of earth taken by the Voyager 1 space probe, in which our mighty planet is a pinprick, a tiny speck of dirt floating in space between ribbons of sunlight. Just like the dust particles that swirled above my head in ballet class. I remember the awe I felt the first time I saw the photo. *How huge is this universe*, I thought to myself, *and how small my life.*

In the same week that the pale blue dot made headlines, Nelson Mandela was released, after spending twenty-seven years in prison for believing that all people deserved to be treated equally. It was February of 1990. Along with the rest of South Africa, and probably the world, I sat glued to the television, watching him walk to freedom on a long dirt road, not far from my mother's childhood farm in Paarl.

With each step, it seemed, came more revelations of the atrocities that had occurred during the apartheid era. It was a tiny glimpse into the cruelty of the system from which I, with my green eyes, Afrikaner mother and English father, had so carelessly benefited my entire life.

These two events engaged in a curious two-step in my mind: that despite the smallness of our individual lives, our capacity for inflicting pain and brutality on others is enormous. But what if we could harness that same power for good?

This would have been the time to claim my father's sword from under the bed. To march into the world and right some wrongs. Fulfil the destiny Father Ignatius, and my name, had bestowed on me. Instead, I got pregnant.

6

Sweet Jesus! The dwarf plunges his sword into the torso of a musketeer almost three times his height. The wounded man falls to the ground in slow motion. Spread-eagled on the cobblestones, his white ruffled sleeve reddens as it lies draped across the brass buckle where the blade entered his body. The miniature murderer removes his hat and sweeps it dramatically across his chest, its purple feather vibrating with victory. The crowd goes wild as he bows grandly. A wave of nausea forces me to the curb.

Nico, Sylvia and I left Güemes two days ago. And while I'm deeply thankful to have escaped mass poisoning, things are going steadily downhill. My Achilles is no better. My position as the caboose in our little group allows me to stretch out the offending tendon at the beginning of each walk, without Nico and Sylvia noticing. And then I focus on what a gritty pilgrim I am. I keep my tears for the shower at the end of the day. That way only God sees them.

But more than my ankle today, it's the people in Santillana del Mar that are making me feel sick. The ancient village, where we arrived a few hours ago, would be gorgeous were it not stuffed to breaking point with people. We seem to have arrived during some kind of festival. Hundreds of tourists, in fancy shoes and freshly-laundered clothes, clutter the cobblestone courtyards. Roaming amongst them are performers, dressed in ruffled shirts and waistcoats, with brightly-coloured sashes across their shoulders. They wear leather boots and belts with intricately engraved buckles. Musketeer-style hats complete their outfits, with feathers so long and lush that they seem to have lives of their own, dancing in the sunlight. Each musketeer carries a sword, completely convincing in its ability to mortally wound.

I have become separated from Sylvia and Nico. They will never find me down here, but my sore ankle and my queasiness are keeping me rooted to the ground.

The wounded giant in front of me still has not moved. The crimson stain spreading across his torso makes my stomach gurgle, so I turn away. Wrought-iron balconies overlooking the courtyard all bear clay pots overflowing with identical fuchsia-coloured flowers. They remind me of the decorative stage balconies from the ballets of my childhood. *Romeo and Juliet. Coppélia.*

Usually I love make-believe. But make-believe is for the dark, not for the stark brightness of day in the middle of a pilgrimage. Performances are sacred, to be appreciated with awe. Without the intrusions of real life, like swollen ankles and nausea. They need shadows and mystery. Magic. Like the nights at the Opera House with my father.

My father was one of ten children. One day his mother quietly walked out the door, abandoning her brood. The siblings were separated and my father and two of his brothers ended up in an orphanage. At least, that's the way the story has been told to me. And not by my father. He never spoke of it. But I sometimes wonder how that affected the kind of father he became – one who saw only goodness in his daughters, steadfastly believing they could do no wrong.

He was a superb athlete and was blessed with a daughter, me, who had zero hand-eye coordination and the speed of a sloth. But instead of bemoaning his fate, he embraced my universe of satin ribbons and hair accessories and delighted in taking me to every ballet that came to town. I'm not sure that he actually enjoyed *Swan Lake* or *The Nutcracker,* but he knew how much I loved this pretend-world where anything could happen.

Over the years there were many highlights: *A Midsummer Night's Dream, Giselle, Don Quixote.* But the performance that will stay with me always is Maina Gielgud's *Squeaky Door.* I was thirteen and all the ballerinas I had seen up to this point were sylph-like creatures, more like graceful stick insects than flesh-and-blood human beings. I was mesmerised by Maina. Not soft or fairylike, she was pure strength and determination. A warrior in a white unitard, she danced to squeaks and creaks, balancing her sinewy self on one pointe shoe for what seemed like eternity. Every muscle rippled with graceful ferocity, her arms and torso tautly precise in a way that seemed both completely familiar and horribly foreign. The sharply discordant creaks and the angles her body made took my breath away. It was so unexpected, so brash, so unconventional.

During a pause between creaks, my father leaned towards me and whispered, "You can do this."

It would take another few years for the harsh reality of not being good enough to sink in, but that night, in the dark, I imagined I could. Because my father said so.

Had he lived as long as he should have, he would, I'm sure, have been in the audience during my burlesque foray, and his would have been the loudest applause. Because that's the kind of father he was.

Sylvia finds me as the crowd starts dispersing, in search of the next bloodthirsty performance in a different courtyard. The dead man still does not move.

"You OK?" she asks.

I nod, not wanting to be *that* pilgrim, complaining about my precious ankle or over-population. She sits beside me, unperturbed by the fake blood trickling towards us, and opens her Camino Bible.

"There is an old saying that Santillana del Mar is the Town of Three Lies," she reads. "Because it is neither a Saint (Santo), nor flat (llana), nor by the sea (Mar) as its name implies."

Sylvia is an enigma. Nearly ten years younger than Nico and thirty years younger than me, she is the unquestioned leader of our little pilgrim pack. In many ways she seems older than me. Wiser, certainly. I want to know more about her, but I suspect it will take longer than the time we'll have together for me to earn her trust. She wears her guidebook like a suit of armour. In the five days that we have been together, she has not volunteered any personal information. I don't even know whether she has siblings. Or parents. Under normal circumstances this would drive me dilly, spending this long with someone and not asking questions. But there are many things I don't want to speak about either. *Tit for tat* my mother would say. So I don't pry.

Another surge of nausea. The sun is too bright and my eyes are watering even though I'm wearing the ugly bucket hat – my husband's parting gift to me. Sylvia stands, offering me her hand, guidebook tucked into her armpit, and we join the stream of tourists.

A large sign with a bright pink background grabs my attention. A wimpled nun with cat-green eyes peers at me from between large white flowery letters on the poster. Her lips are disturbingly plump.

"What does it say?" I ask.

"It's advertising cookies." Sylvia is the only one in our family-of-three who speaks Spanish. "It says they contain no colourants or preservatives but are a divine pleasure. Do you see what they're called?"

"Tetillas de monja?" I read out loud. "What does that mean?"

"Nun's tits," she laughs.

These I need to see! Ignoring the warning gurgles in my stomach, I enter the store. Sylvia follows. It's dark inside. As my eyes adjust I make out the mounds of baked breasts, so pale they could only belong to nuns. Or vampires. Each cookie bears, in its centre, a perfectly-proportioned pink nipple. Art, really. I buy six, hoping that my nausea is simply hunger.

While Sylvia goes in search of Nico, I find a bench in the church square. It is quiet and cool. The tourists have somehow not found this place. I take one pale breast from the brown baggie. It's sweet and creamy and melts in my mouth. *If Sister Bernadette could see me now.* I eat every last nipple.

There is still no one else around and I stretch out on the bench, making the most of this haven of peace in an otherwise over-touristed town. My eyelids, heavy with sugar, close. The day seems not so terrible anymore.

And then the explosion. I shoot upright on the bench. People are streaming out of the church, filling the square. Has there been some kind of attack? More explosions! Why aren't they running away? *I should run away!* What are they doing? Why are they laughing?

And then I see them – fireworks! And on the church steps a bride and groom. It's a wedding. The people in front of the church form two lines, creating a passageway for the newlyweds, showering them with pink petals. They are close enough for me to see the beads of sweat on the groom's upper lip, the excitement in his bride's eyes.

The next explosion triggers something inside me, and in front of hundreds of glamorous wedding guests, I vomit. Holding onto my bucket hat, I spit every last nun's tit onto the cobblestones. With the back of my hand, I wipe my mouth and then try to find my way back to the albergue.

It's getting dark, and as I get closer, I hear the neighs. I can't see the horses, but I can smell them. As the hostel comes into view, I step in a mound of poop. My foot slips away from me, the swollen ankle making a nasty clicking sound. *Ouch!*

I head for the shower thinking about the bride whose parade I just rained on. She with the white, white dress of hope and flowers of ever-after in her hair. Does she understand the enormity of what she's done, binding herself to someone else for the rest of her life?

What I remember most vividly about my own wedding day, is waiting outside the Presbyterian Church on Caledon Street in George, my husband's hometown. At the end of the pathway, two wooden doors stood guard. On the other side of those doors, everyone was waiting. For me.

Something flickered in my spine, like the Guy Fawkes Day sparklers from my childhood. Every year, on the fifth of November, we kids would run through the neighbourhood gardens, making fantastically complicated, glittery patterns with our sparklers. Circles. Figure eights. Messages written in luminous letters that danced then faded. Like shooting stars. Wishes.

At some point, someone would scream and we'd drop the little burning sticks instantly. We had been warned that we would lose our fingers if we held on too long. I'd watch my sparkler writhing in the grass – all that shimmering magic with nowhere to go. And then it would stop moving. Dead. When I picked it up to throw it in the trash, I was always sad to see how much of it was unburned. Unused. All that sparkle wasted. And I would wish that I'd held on longer.

Standing outside the church on my wedding day felt somehow the same. And then I noticed the cracks in the cement, zig-zagging around my toes in every direction.

I'm not sure where I first heard about the bad luck that lay in wait beneath the cracks. Maybe from one of the neighbourhood children. Maybe it was while we were watching our dying sparklers thrashing about on the ground. Maybe not. But I knew the only way to avoid that bad luck, was to never step on a crack. Touching it, with even one tiny part of one tiny toenail, could unleash the most terrible things.

And there, outside the church on Caledon Street, were so many cracks, I didn't know where to step. My father took my arm and looped it through his. It felt like the time in the darkened theatre, watching Maina, when he'd whispered to me, *you can do this.* Then he steered me across the web of all-the-things-that-could-go-badly, towards the promise waiting for me at the end of the aisle. I did not look down. Just in case.

7

The sun rising behind us illuminates the road ahead as we leave Santillana del Mar for Comillas, our next stop on the Way. With the tourists all still asleep in their fancy hotels, it feels like a pilgrimage again. I lag behind a little so that Nico and Sylvia can't see my awkward sideways crab walk up the hill. They are ahead of me as we pass the church square where I threw up yesterday. Someone must have cleaned up my mess, because there is not one regurgitated nipple in sight.

The cobblestones are littered with pink petals, now crushed by hundreds of tourist feet. Sylvia turns round as I reach down to gather some of the broken pinkness. She waits for me, leaving Nico, for the first time, the leader.

"How do you know when you've met *the one*?" she asks when I reach her.

"I don't think there *is* a one," I say, peeking at the petals in my palm. "My grandmother believed there was."

The little I know about my maternal grandfather I learned from Ouma. After marrying, they lived an idyllic rural life, adventuring in the vineyards and orchards, along the river and in the mountains. Until the day he died of a heart attack, at age forty-four, leaving my grandmother to take care of the farm and four young children on her own. Her husband had been her one true love. Her soulmate. In sickness and in health, and long after death parted them.

"After he died, she spent the next fifty years on her own," I tell Sylvia. "What's the point of a love like that? It's stupid, if you ask me."

Sylvia sighs. And I am suddenly remorseful. Have I dashed her hopes? Is there someone in Venice, waiting for her? Is Sylvia's pilgrimage also a *walk first, decide later* affair? We catch up with Nico and the moment is lost. I want to kick myself. What if there isn't another opportunity to find out what Sylvia's big question is? I am *such* a bad pilgrim. I need to fix this, so I say, "But I don't understand love, Sylvia, so don't listen to me."

"What's to understand?" Nico chimes in, picking up the tail end of the conversation.

I can't answer, because how do I explain that my feelings run wide, not deep. My teenage-self believed that this was how Jesus loved – everyone a little, no-one too much. But Jesus wasn't a wife. My inability to say the word, out loud, has become something of a joke between me and my husband. He tells me he loves me, and I say thank-you. It would be hilarious if it wasn't so sad. *Thank-you.*

Sylvia opens her mouth, as if to say something, but Nico interrupts: "Why *did* you get married?"

Nico asked me this question in Güemes and I can't brush it off again, so I tell him about the baby.

When we found out about the pregnancy, my husband-to-be turned it into an excuse for a party. He invited our closest friends and family members to join us in tying the knot. A wedding didn't fit my plans of making my way through the world on my own, guided by the voice of God and my father's sword. But a baby needed a family. Everyone knew that.

A week before the big day I found a salon and asked for a very short cut. As my hair piled up on the floor, I started crying. The stylist flung his arms in the air, holding the scissors above my head, as if they, on their own, were responsible for this disaster.

"Keep going," I sobbed.

"You sure?"

I nodded. I wasn't sad because I no longer had hair. My tears were because of what was staring back at me from the mirror: noble cheekbones, electric eyes. Fire. A knight-in-shining-armour. The person I was meant to be.

I heard my mother's voice in my head. *Pull yourself towards yourself.* I'd never really understood what that meant. But the expression on her face, each time she said it, was clear. *Be grateful. Things could be worse.*

So, sitting in that red vinyl salon chair, seven days before my wedding, I pulled myself towards myself, and focused on the things for which I should be grateful. Family. Health. Sunshine. Someone who was willing to marry me. By the time the stylist laid down the last of his shearing tools, I'd stopped crying. There was a dress to be collected.

Despite taking biology all the way through high school, I never learned about the human reproductive system. Sister Bernadette had omitted this part of the syllabus. I suppose the reasoning was that if you didn't talk about sex, it wouldn't happen. And because my focus had always been on matters of the spirit, I hadn't paid much attention to the workings of my body. I didn't know how much or how quickly my pregnant insides would expand. So when the time came to find a wedding dress, I thought a drop waist would be safest. Of course, it couldn't be white. That would simply compound my sin. It would be like laughing in God's face. The tent-like turquoise option seemed to be the logical solution.

But in an ironic twist, I no longer needed the drop waist by the time I walked down the aisle. Two days after my haircut, I woke up with severe stomach cramps. Later, in the hospital, the baby was floated away in a river of blood.

"There's no reason you won't go on to have many more healthy pregnancies," the doctor said, after my uterus had been scraped sparkly clean. "Miscarriages are quite common." That word again.

We went ahead and got married. Sixty odd people were expecting a party. There was no time to change the dress.

"So how long have you been married?" Nico asks.

"Almost twenty-five years."

"Then I guess there was more to it than just being pregnant," he says.

Oh. We walk in silence for the next twenty kilometres. It's one of the peculiarities of the Camino – this understanding of when to speak and when to be silent. I wish the real world worked this way too.

Just outside the albergue in Comillas is a signpost with arrows. It's 1820 kilometres to Rome and 5170 to Jerusalem. The only distance I'm interested in, is Santiago: 455 kilometres. Still a long way to go.

Our accommodation tonight was originally the city jail, built in 1879, but the dungeons and courtyard have since been converted to sleep pilgrims. Only twenty. And it's a good thing that we left Santillana as early as we did this morning, because the pilgrims who arrive after us are turned away. It's full tonight. No room at the prison.

The hospitalero who stamps our credenciales tells us that Comillas was once the capital of Spain. In 1881, the first Marquis de Comillas, Antonio López y López, invited his friend, King Alfonso XII, to visit his home. Alfonso had become king of Spain in 1874, at just seventeen years of age. In preparation for the royal visit, Comillas was adorned and transformed. When the king and his family arrived, thirty lanterns were illuminated, making Comillas the first Spanish town to have electric streetlighting. A celebration, attended by the king, some generals, and the congress of ministers, was the reason for Comillas becoming the capital of Spain – for only one day. I sincerely hope Alfonso appreciated the effort.

The hospitalero returns our credenciales and I deposit Petunia on my bunk upstairs, before leaving again to find the cathedral. It's Father's Day and I have a candle to light.

The church is easy to find. There is no-one else inside. In a darkened alcove, Jesus is nailed to a cross, ribs protruding above his loincloth, black sockets for eyes. He makes me feel guilty, so I find a pew where he can't see me. Genuflecting awkwardly, my ankle twinging, I kneel in front of Mary.

I suffer from prayer anxiety. It started during high school. Before every test I would light a candle in the school chapel. Then I'd kneel in the front row and pray for clarity of mind. I never prayed for an A, because I didn't want God to think I was selfish. There were other things going on in the world: people starving, dying, losing body parts to leprosy. So instead, I asked him to help me remember everything I'd learned, which was, well, everything. As a teenager, nothing was left to chance. I always hoped though, that God, being God and all, would be able to hear between the lines and understand that it was really an A that I needed.

Hail Mary, full of grace, the Lord is with thee. Comillas Mary interrupts my prayers with her fluorescent halo and three strands of flickering lights dripping from each of her palms. With their pale blue glow, she seems more like a lady of the night than the mother of our Saviour. I close my eyes, trying to shut them out. *Blessed art thou amongst women, and blessed is the fruit of thy womb, Jesus.* But this is the kind of gaudy that just begs you to stare. It wouldn't surprise me to find fishnet stockings under her flouncy stone dress.

Unable to focus, I light a candle for my father and leave the church, hobbling back up the hill. Sylvia is reading on a little patch of grass outside the albergue. She points to an enormous statue overlooking the ocean.

"Wow, what *is* that?"

"The Angel of Death," she says, telling me about Joseph Llimona's magnificent work of sculpture, the Exterminating Angel, that stands watch over the cemetery.

"I'll see you later." I have to visit the angel.

"What about dinner?"

"Could you keep me some fruit?" A good graveyard will trump dinner every time. There is nowhere quite as peaceful, or more likely to provide perspective on life's little dramas. Being surrounded by tombstones is a reminder that simply being alive is cause for celebration. And the bonus is that dead people don't judge.

I inherited my love of graveyards from my grandmother. From the time that I could toddle, Ouma would take me to visit our dead relatives, where they lay buried in the shadow of Paarl mountain. The two of us spent hours wandering through the gravestones, leaving trails of flowers, as she told me the family stories. When we got to my grandfather's grave – the one I never met –

Ouma would point to the space waiting for her beside her beloved husband and tell me how much she was looking forward to someday joining him for all eternity. It was a beautiful story when I was a child. Romantic. But as I got older, I wondered about the wisdom of loving one person so ferociously.

Ouma would have loved this seaside cemetery. The white angel's eyes burn with intent and veins pop on his sculpted forearms as he scans the Cantabrian Sea. Body angled in concentration, wings outstretched, he stands guard amidst the Gothic ruins. He holds a sword in one hand, and with the other leans back onto a tombstone, as if gathering strength for what is to come. It's my father's sword! Again.

The sun sinks into the sea and it's suddenly dark. How long have I been here?

Everyone is in bed by the time I get back. Sylvia has left an apple on my pillowcase, and I pop it into Petunia's side pocket. Sliding into my sleeping bag, I imagine the Exterminating Angel accompanying me as I walk, my father's sword tucked under his arm.

My destiny is around the corner. I can feel it.

Happy Father's Day, Pa.

8

Serdio is only twenty-one kilometres away from Comillas, a relatively short day, but it's already hot. Today's route takes us through a natural park. My ankle is feeling worse, despite the beauty all around me and the absence of asphalt.

I'm relieved when we reach Serdio. It is peaceful. And picturesque. Green fields, cows in pasture, the occasional rooster. No traffic. Sylvia's guidebook lists the population as fifty-two.

My delight is short-lived. The albergue is an off-white concrete rectangle with slashes of dirty yellow paint on the exterior. A dilapidated Lego house with an orange roof, there are bars on either side of the front door. Inside, an antiseptic smell is surely camouflaging something sinister. The air tastes like madness. I shower as quickly as I can, wearing my flip flops to avoid contamination. There's more than enough Crazy in my life already.

"I'm heading to the store," Nico says, as I hang my towel out to dry. "Coming?"

The general store, a small concrete block, is situated in a dust bowl, where three dirt roads meet. Nico and I grab ice creams from the rusty freezer and sit under the faded umbrella, watching pilgrims shuffle in to Serdio. What has drawn all these people, from so many different places, backgrounds, ages, circumstances, to become pilgrims? Are they, like me, seeking some kind of forgiveness? Divine assistance?

When I first read *The Canterbury Tales* in English class, I learned that pilgrimages were acts of penance. By becoming a pilgrim, sins could be forgiven. Four places were noted, in *The Catholic Encyclopedia*, as being suitable for atoning for particularly serious crimes: the body of Saint Thomas at Canterbury, the Three Kings' relics at Cologne, the tomb of the Apostles in Rome and Saint James' shrine in Santiago de Compostela.

And while pilgrimages did have dangers associated with them – getting lost, starving, being attacked, robbed, dying – they were also opportunities for revelry. During the Middle Ages, going on vacation was not an option. There was, however, dispensation for going on a pilgrimage. It was the one legitimate activity that could set you free from the drudgery of everyday life.

Is it any different today? I have taken three weeks out of my life – my family's life – to be a pilgrim. I have told myself that I am walking towards God. And myself. But what if I'm simply walking *away*? Nothing noble at all. Only an escape.

"How are your feet?" Nico interrupts.

"OK, thanks." It's not really a lie. My feet are fine. It's my Achilles that's the problem.

"Blisters?" He's not going to give up so easily.

"Little bit," I say, feeling the bubbles forming between my toes.

"I've got blister needles. Let's go get you one."

You get blister needles?

Back at the albergue, I examine my feet in the courtyard. Sliding one of Nico's needles smoothly into one very puffy bubble, I feel like a surgeon. The heat between my toes instantly evaporates. *Oh wow.* How much liquid can one blister hold? The magic needle goes into the garbage, Nico insisting it's only good for one use. I don't want to end up in hospital with infected toes. *Not* reaching Santiago de Compostela is not an option. That's where God's waiting.

I collect my towel from the washing line. The boy at Mountain Equipment Co-op was right – it really does dry almost instantly! And then I start my evening preparations. Pilgrim etiquette discourages early-morning noise, so before I go to sleep at night everything is ready for a quick and quiet departure the next day. When I wake up, all I have to do is peel off the shirt I have slept in and slip on my sports bra, T-shirt and shorts. I do all this without leaving my bunk. I have noticed that most of the peregrinas – the lady pilgrims – change in the bathroom. They have obviously not stripped in public before.

Once I'm dressed, my toes get new princess Band-Aids. Then it's socks and shoes, roll up the sleeping bag, and off to the bathroom. I'm not a breakfast person, so I'm ready to go as soon as I've brushed my teeth and filled my water bottle. The most liberating thing about being a pilgrim is not washing my face or combing my hair in the morning. The just-in-case mascara remains unopened, somewhere inside Petunia.

There are eight bunks in the room tonight. Sixteen pilgrims. I still haven't figured out why this place is making me so edgy. Maybe it's the starkness. The aridity. As if some deranged creature snuck in and stole all the hope. And whatever once existed shriveled up because no one cared enough to keep it alive.

Tomorrow can't come soon enough.

Where the hell is everyone this morning? I can't imagine anyone
got any sleep last night – except those responsible for the
horrendous snoring. While I wait for Nico and Sylvia, I
stretch my ankle, very, very carefully. Serdio is the last place
I want to be stuck with a snapped tendon.

"Jesus Christ," says Nico as he joins me. "Those
fucking snorers. You shouldn't be allowed to sleep with
human beings if you make noises like that."

Like ballet, sleeping in albergues is not for the faint of
heart. When Sylvia steps through the door, her eyes
bloodshot, she doesn't say anything, not even hello, and we
walk in silence in our usual formation: Sylvia leading the
way, Nico following, and me trailing behind, content not
to know where I am going. How quickly we have
established our rules of engagement. How did we each
assume our individual roles in our little pilgrim family?
With no discussion. Is this how we fall into our lives? A
whisper here. A glance there. And before you know it,
spirals of self-fulfilling prophecies become us?

When Sylvia eventually speaks, it's at a sign in the road.
"We have a choice now," she says. "Highway or beach."

"Which way is shorter?" Nico asks.

"Highway."

"Highway it is." Nico leaves no room for discussion. I
could kiss him. My Achilles needs the shortest route
possible. Thankfully my toes, newly nestled in Ariel and
Snow White Band-Aids, are not complaining today. Nico's
blister needle seems to have done the trick.

The yellow line on the side of the road is interrupted at
regular intervals by a painted scallop shell, confirmation
that we are on the right track. What did medieval pilgrims
do? They had no signage. No hostels with bunk-beds and
washrooms. No fancy walking shoes or blister needles.
And assuming they were lucky enough to reach their

destination without succumbing to disease or murder, they had to turn around and do it all over again. Just backwards and more exhausted.

We almost miss the arrow. Pendueles. The path to the ocean is rocky and steep. My feet keep sliding away from me. Focused on the ground below my shoes, I don't look up until I'm safely at the bottom. *Mother of God.* It's the rock from my dream. All that's missing is the chair. And my father.

A few weeks after striding into holy matrimony, my new husband and I decided to postpone real life. With the baby gone, there was nothing shackling us to adulthood. So we sold our few possessions, bought two backpacks and headed for Europe. The backpacks were khaki. They did not have names.

It was the early nineties. Communication with friends and family in South Africa was via postcards and public telephones. We moved slowly west, making our way to Canada, and four months after leaving home a ferry deposited us on Vancouver Island. We were camping in a town called Nanaimo when my father visited me in my dreams one night. He was sitting in a wooden chair on a flat rock. As I walked towards him, he started dissolving, melting through the seat's criss-cross strips of leather, a human waterfall evaporating into mist as it hit the rock. I woke up drenched and went in search of a telephone.

"Aunty Bettie, it's Lindy-Lou."

While my childhood friend, Samantha, and I had drifted apart, I knew Aunty Bettie would know what was going on at home. More important, she would tell me the truth.

"I dreamt about my father. How is he?" I asked, leaning against the cool glass door of the public phone booth.

Silence.

"Aunty Bettie?" Maybe I'd lost the connection.

"You should come home," she said.

So I did. But before I got back, my father was dead. My plane landed just in time for his cremation. I did not cry. That night, in my dreams, I put a baby in a backpack. I thought I was doing a good thing, protecting him from all the evil in the world. But I forgot where I put the backpack. I searched everywhere. When I eventually found it, under a rug in a shadowy corner of the garage, the baby was curled into a tiny ball, absolutely still. Like an unshelled snail. Two days later I found out I was pregnant. Again.

Nine months after my father died, our son was born. Twenty-two months later, a day before our third wedding anniversary, our daughter arrived. We settled in George – the town where my husband had grown up and where we had got married. It was a pretty place, framed on one side by a mountain range, and on the other by long sandy beaches and the wild waves of the Indian Ocean.

My husband travelled a lot for work in those early years. So, in unspoken agreement, I stayed home with our children while he flew about, providing for our needs. Those who say motherhood comes naturally are liars. I have never felt like a real mother. My only superpower was feeling my children's pain. An extra pair of eyes or half-decent cooking skills would have been far more useful.

Because I wasn't sure what regular mothers did, my children and I spent a lot of time under the banana trees in the garden, inventing cloud stories, painting rocks and eating raw vegetables. I vaguely recall a blue potty on the lawn. My version of toilet training.

What I do remember is the beach. Almost every morning, regardless of the weather, the three of us set off to collect shells and build sandcastles. And every afternoon, we read fairy tales on the king-size bed that my husband and I didn't share very much.

If I close my eyes I can still feel the weight of their little heads on my chest as I read *The Magic Faraway Tree* and *The Wishing Chair*. I loved my children, but I had no idea what I was doing. My plan was simply to try to keep them alive until they could fend for themselves. And I almost didn't succeed in doing that.

When our son was five and our daughter three, we decided it was time for an adventure. Canada was a land of opportunity and could provide our children with the safety and security that seemed to be disappearing in South Africa. We sold almost everything we owned, packing only books, the shells we had collected on the beach, and Ouma's antique chair, the one my father had used for his dreamtime visit before he died. On a rock just like this one in Pendueles.

There are other people on the beach here, but I'm in no mood for small talk. While Nico and Sylvia introduce themselves, I hobble towards the strangely familiar rock, marveling at how birth, death, love, loss and guilt dance together. Forever. I sit cross-legged on the rock, watching the growing group of pilgrims silhouetted in the dusk. There is a stirring inside me. A reminder of the Crazy. That I am here for a reason. This is not a holiday. I am not a tourist. I am a pilgrim. And my pilgrimage is not going as planned. Tomorrow when we reach Llanes, I will say goodbye to Nico and Sylvia and take the bus to Lugo and the Camino Primitivo.

To walk alone. As it was intended.

9

Indulging in existential crises is the birthright of the privileged.

It was a latté that triggered my crisis. I tripped over the dog and my coffee ended up on the off-white living room rug. Under normal circumstances, a spilled beverage would not send me over the edge. But Leonard Cohen was singing about light and dark and bells ringing. And signs. He was singing about doves and freedom. And cracks. He was singing about me.

So, that Wednesday morning, in my navy-blue Eagle Harbour cottage, with the mini-van in the driveway, the sun shining on the magnolias, and Leonard singing my life, I indulged. I had put my destiny on hold for marriage, motherhood and life in the suburbs. And I had done it willingly, with just a dash of martyrdom. But now I was faced with the irrefutable fact that I had done *nothing* with my life.

I'm not sure how long I stood there, sobbing, watching the stain spread, turning the white rug black. The dog whimpered. The cat slunk away. Leonard sang. My weeping continued – loud and ugly.

Pull yourself towards yourself. My mother's words had worked before, and they worked this time too. The coffee would not miraculously climb back into the mug. Not even Jesus managed to do that, did he? I went in search of the carpet cleaner.

Later that night, coffee stain more-or-less removed, family fed, dishes done, house in relative order, I sank into bed. As my head hit the pillow, everything I had *not* done flashed before me.

The voice of reason that lives somewhere in my frontal lobes screamed at me through my suburban angst. *The world is filled with victims of violent crimes,* it yelled, *people imprisoned in poverty, unable to feed their children, incapable of paying for medication that could improve their quality of life, women with no education, abusive partners, no way of escaping the political turmoil in which they live. Those women have no time for a midlife crisis. Every day is a crisis. A real one. Now get over yourself!*

I ignored the voice. This was no time for logic. Instead, faced with all that unlived life, I got up and cleaned the fridge, the stove, every wine glass we owned. I rearranged furniture. And then I found the kitchen scissors. How hard could it be to cut your own hair? Ten minutes later, staring at my reflection in the bathroom mirror, the answer to that question was clear.

The next day, I crossed Lions Gate bridge in search of a professional to fix the mess on my head. I found Lila in a funky salon close to the Seabus terminal. She was dressed entirely in black. Tiny neon skulls glowed from each of her black fingernails. She had just had a cancellation. I made myself comfortable in the scratched-up leather chair in front of Lila's mirror.

"I cut it myself," I apologised.

"That's a relief," she smiled, revealing one gold incisor. "So I don't have to recommend that you sue your last stylist."

I laughed. We would get along just fine even though she looked no older than twelve.

"What are we doing?" she asked, as if I would somehow be involved in the process.

"Whatever you want." I was tired of making decisions.

Lila brought me a pile of magazines and rotated my chair away from the mirror. Forty-five minutes later, just as I was starting to panic about my parking expiring, she turned me around again.

Sweet Jesus.

"So?" Lila asked.

I leaned toward my reflection. While it wasn't as short as my wedding day pixie cut, it had done the same for my eyes and my cheekbones. I looked alive again. As though I had a *purpose*. Lila had shaped my hair tightly around my head, with wispy bits around my jaw. Something shifted in my spine. A new kind of energy. Sparkly.

"I love it." I really wanted to tell Lila I loved *her.*

Still trying to name the frolicking in my vertebrae, I left the salon. It was unusually hot for March in Vancouver, and the stray hairs were making my neck itch. I drove back across the bridge with all the windows open, the rearview mirror angled to see myself. My neck was angry red. Was that why my eyes were so bright?

I parked the mini-van in the driveway and went to collect the mail. A horn honked. It was Adam. We had met through one of my son's sports teams and our paths had crossed a few times over the years. I waved, dropping the Hydro bill. He slowed down, parked his red convertible across the street and by the time I'd picked up the envelope he was standing next to me.

"Hey," he said. "Long time, no see." His smile was dazzling, the kind of dazzling you found in fashion magazines, not in driveways in the suburbs.

"Hi." I hoped my tie-dye T-shirt was camouflaging the sweat trickling down my stomach. I think we chatted about our summer plans, the kids, his work. But I can't be sure. His closeness kept interrupting my focus. He didn't seem to need as much personal space as I did.

"I should go," he said after a while. "Nice to see you. You're looking good." He leaned in to hug me which was confusing. And made me anxious. Did I smell bad?

"You too," I replied stiffly.

Adam moved away as if to go, then turned back towards me, taking a step closer, right into my space bubble. I actually felt it pop.

"I've always been attracted to you," he said matter-of-factly into my strawberry neck, as if it didn't matter in the least that we were both married to other people. Or that he was gorgeous. Or younger than me. My stomach was burning up. Was he trying to make a fool of me? What did that even mean? Attracted to you? I had visions of bees and wildflowers. *Say something goddammit!* Completely flustered, all I could say was "thank-you." *Not again!*

The driveway palaver resembled, all too closely, another embarrassing 'thank-you' when I was thirteen, in front of Father Ray, wearing a hideous white ruffle dress. My friend, Lee-Anne, was right beside me. She was not wearing a hideous ruffle dress because, unlike me, she had taste.

We'd endured evening Bible study classes once a week for months and were, at last, being rewarded with First Communion. We did not yet know that ours was a second-rate communion, that the bread and wine in the Methodist Church was only pretending to be Christ's body and blood.

Father Ray put the wafer in my hand and I said "thank-you." I may even have popped a little curtsey. Lee-Anne snort-giggled. I turned red. I didn't know that you weren't meant to say thank-you. Wasn't that rude? Lee-Anne told me later that communion protocol was to "say nothing."

I wish I'd remembered the communion incident before I said thank-you to Adam in the driveway. But once I'd said it, I couldn't unsay it, so I blushed. Exactly as I had in front of Father Ray and God Almighty, more than thirty years ago.

"I'll call you. Let's go for lunch soon," he said, magnanimously ignoring my scorched cheeks.

"OK." *What!?*

"Cheers." He sauntered off, leaving me in a sweaty pile of angst next to the cedar tree. Had any of the neighbours seen us? According to my mother and Aunty Bettie, this wasn't the way things worked. I did not dress like someone who encouraged other people's husbands to walk into my driveway. I never wore too-tight shirts and I didn't even own a skirt. Adam must have been kidding. *Pulling your leg,* my father would have said.

I shook my newly-cut head like a traumatised dog and pushed the awkward driveway dance from my mind. The little serpent sashayed up my spinal cord. It was the same feeling I'd had when I saw myself in the salon mirror earlier. It felt like glitter. Promise.

Waking up in my little bunk in Pendueles this morning, it is with a similar sense of anticipation. As if something is about to happen. But it's accompanied with sadness. Today is my last day with Nico and Sylvia. And I still know almost nothing about them.

The three of us leave early, before the other pilgrims get started. The road takes us through a grassy meadow, then downhill through a stream so dry that we don't need the bridge that was built to cross it.

As I start to crave café con leche, we find a little café. We dump our packs under the awning on the spotless stone floor. How often must it be swept to stay this clean?

The tables, with their red-and-green checkered cloths, look out on the pale purple mountains in the distance. This is the last breakfast coffee I'll share with these two human beings who have walked with me for nearly three hundred kilometres. In the very early hours of tomorrow morning, long before sunrise, a bus will take me to Lugo, four hundred kilometres away, where I'll be joining the Camino Primitivo.

While we drink our coffee, Sylvia tells me that the Primitivo is the Original Way. "It was the first Camino route and King Alfonso II was the first pilgrim to walk it in the ninth century."

Little Alfonso was born in the year 760. His father was King Fruela I. His mother, Munía, had been captured by his father while he was at war with the Basques. Fruela was a violent man, who killed his brother, which subsequently resulted in his own assassination, when Alfonso was only eight years old. So much for an untroubled childhood.

The new king, Aurelio, was throned by the nobles who had killed Fruela. Six years later, Aurelio died and the crown reverted to Alfonso's uncle, Silo. King Silo and his wife Adonisa, brought fourteen-year-old Alfonso to live with them in their palace in Oviedo and for the next nine years Alfonso learned the ins-and-outs of the court. King Silo died in 783 without any heirs, and the nobles, under pressure from Adoniso, chose Alfonso as his successor. But a few months later, Mauregato usurped the throne. He was the illegitimate son of Alfonso's grandfather, Alfonso

I and Muslim slave Sisalda. Alfonso fled, taking refuge with his dead mother's parents in Álava. When Mauregato died, Alfonso returned from exile, becoming king at the age of thirty-one.

Alfonso II lived an austere life, in strict accordance with Christian morality. Known as Alfonso the Chaste, he did eventually take a wife, but never consummated his marriage. It was during his reign that Saint James' remains were found, and it was Alfonso II who built the chapel to safeguard those remains. Over time, that chapel became the cathedral in Santiago de Compostela, the very same one I am walking towards.

Sylvia lists the recommended pilgrim supplies for the Primitivo. It bears very little resemblance to what's inside Petunia.

"A snake-bite kit?" I ask. "Do either of you have one?"

Nico doesn't. Sylvia does. The guidebook says there are thirteen different types of snakes in Spain, five that are fatal to humans.

"Oh, they're exaggerating," Sylvia says. "There's only one snake that can kill you. It lives in the mountains. And I don't think the Primitivo goes through the mountains. Anyway, snakes are very shy." The book agrees – a snake will only attack if it feels threatened. Unfortunately, it doesn't give any tips on how *not* to threaten a snake.

We finish our coffee and continue on to Llanes. The clifftop path winds between long grass and the ocean stretches out below us as far as we can see. The scenery is strikingly similar to the first day the three of us walked together, from Pobeña. That was ten days ago. Ten days! Half my pilgrimage!

I will miss my pilgrim family. But it has to be done. I have to walk alone. And I am thrilled to be following in the footsteps of the very first pilgrim. I feel newly pious and pilgrim-ly. Alfonso the Chaste and me.

Our walk into Llanes is light and cheery. Even my ankle is less achy. The albergue we check into is a converted railway station, with high ceilings and an enormous dining room. We spend the evening cooking dinner, laughing, enjoying the space all to ourselves. It's only when I'm drying the last dish that I notice the giant crack running the length of the floor. How many times have I stood in it tonight? What bad luck have I unwittingly unleashed? And how soon will it befall me?

CAMINO PRIMITIVO

*"Those who were seen dancing were thought to be insane
by those who could not hear the music."*
~Friedrich Nietzsche

10

Our father, who art in Heaven, hallowed be thy name. A flare of light punctures my prayer in the cathedral in Lugo, where the bus dropped me not too long ago. I scan the church for its source. High above me, so high that I can barely see it, is a kind of primitive skylight. As the sun shifts, the rays shimmy across the elaborate pillars behind the altar. Six of them. *Thy kingdom come, thy will be done*, I try again. *Good Lord!* Jesus Christ reclines against one of the pillars. Wearing only a loosely-wrapped loincloth, his left hand reaches across his torso, fingers caressing the pale green marble. This is not del Norte Jesus, with exposed ribs and haunted eyes. This Jesus is curvaceous and seductive. The lush drapes around his raised podium are the same deep red as those in the Opera House of my first ballet recital. Jesus' eyes reflect a kind of sultry coyness. *I know your secret*, he seems to be saying. *I have one too.*

It's the burlesque look. The one I never quite mastered.

Unlike here in the church, or at the Opera House, there were no velvet curtains the night I became Luna. There were no curtains at all. I waited in the wings of the Wise Hall in East Vancouver, crammed next to a chicken suit draped over a cracked mirror amidst a hodgepodge of props. Was that bad luck? The cracked mirror? I took a step away from it. There was room for only one step.

It had been a long time, but the darkness backstage was familiar. I couldn't see the audience, but I could feel the tug of the invisible cord connecting us. They promised me adoration in exchange for escape. For a few minutes, there would be no bills, no obligations, no unhappy marriages. Just magic.

The blue lights rose, and from my hiding place I spied my prop on the stage: a white cross attached to a black box, creating the illusion of a tombstone. In this, my debut performance, I was a widow dancing on my dead husband's grave. The dance would end with me standing on top of the tombstone, which I had constructed myself, with an electric screwdriver I'd bought from Home Depot for the occasion. What if the cross clunked to the floor halfway through my performance? Or the box fell apart as I stood on it? *Oh God.*

The microphone crackled as the MC started speaking. Here, no one knew my real name. No one's wife or mother, neither saint nor sinner, I had no friends or family in the audience. They didn't know about my secret.

Suddenly focused on a moth spiraling above me, I didn't hear much of my introduction. The moth was flying too close to the exposed bulb and I watched it die. No explosion. No hiss. Completely unspectacular. Just a smattering of dust descending through the air. I didn't see where it hit the ground. Perhaps it didn't. Maybe it simply evaporated into the ethers, as if it never existed.

My momentary sadness at its unexceptional death was interrupted by the MC announcing my name: Luna Blue. Hair sprayed to rigid perfection, face a mask of made-up calm, I breathed deeply to sidestep the terror building in my bones. Wearing thigh high stockings, satin Audrey Hepburn gloves and my seventeen-year-old daughter's very short black dress, I was, at age forty-seven, about to dance in front of an audience for the first time in decades. More accurately, I was about to remove my daughter's little black dress in front of two hundred people. *May the Lord have mercy on us all.*

The music began. "This Night" was performed by an alternative rock band called Black Lab. The bell tolled – my cue. What if I tripped? Or forgot my routine? Made an absolute fool of myself? And then I saw it – a hairline break in the wooden floor. Instantly I was seven again, tiptoeing tentatively across the sidewalk. Then, arm-in-arm with my father outside the Presbyterian Church, as he guided me towards my future.

I had spent a lifetime avoiding the cracks. But in the vortex of almost-forgotten dreams hovering backstage, I raised one stiletto and stood deliberately on the jaggedness. Right. In. It. I inhaled whatever curse was waiting for me and, in a kind of unholy genuflection, bowed to my ankles. Stepping into the spotlight, I knew that after This Night, nothing would be the same.

Please Jesus, don't let me lose a pastie.

I scrutinise Stripper Jesus behind the altar in Lugo, trying to recall the exact sequence of events that led to me dancing nearly-naked in front of strangers.

My husband had told me, a few months earlier, that I was about as seductive as a slug, and I had to agree. Being a martyr, even in the suburbs, was a full-time occupation, and didn't leave much wiggle-room for sexy. But while it would have been convenient to blame him alone, it was slightly more complicated than that. My emptying nest and insomnia probably played a role. And of course the Crazy cavorting through my vertebrae didn't help. If I really think about it, though, it was the mammogram lady's fault.

When I checked in for my annual mammogram, the lady at the front desk asked for the date of my last period. "Just more or less," she said, when I couldn't remember. She handed me a small wall calendar with kittens on the cover. I thumbed backwards through time. Eight months.

"Is that possible?" I interrogated the poor woman. "Isn't that bad?"

"Not at your age," she said.

My age?

"Menses are irregular during perimenopause. Have a seat over there, sweetie."

Sweetie? Menses? Perimenopause? Did she just make that up? It sounded like some kind of takeout chicken dish from Nando's.

Ten minutes later, mammogram concluded, I made a beeline for Starbucks. With an extra-hot Americano Misto and Wi-Fi, I tried to find out what was happening to my body. The words that popped up on my iPhone were distressing. Fatigue. Night sweats. Insomnia. Depression. And then the cherry on the top: decreased sex drive. My husband would be thrilled. What Sister Bernadette and the

Pope had not managed to suppress, perimenopause would utterly extinguish.

In the midst of a hot flush, a little advertisement sashayed across my screen. *Burlesque Classes!* This could be exactly the kind of ridiculousness that would brighten up my completely uninteresting life and allow me to forget, however temporarily, that I was about to become a dried-up old hag.

There should have been trumpets heralding from the heavens, or at the very least a flash of lightning when I clicked on that little sign-up button. But I have noticed that most life-altering events occur quietly, without even the slightest hint of what's coming. Like happily reading your book on the deck while just down the road your child is about to be hit by a car.

Two days after signing up online, I braved Second Narrows bridge, leaving behind the comfort and safety of West Vancouver to enter the shady world of East Van. It was the equivalent of the wrong side of the tracks of my South African childhood and I could almost hear my ballet teacher hyperventilating as I tiptoed up the linoleum steps to the studio. I was careful not to touch the handrail.

There were eight of us, all the other women in their twenties. If I'd known what was coming, I would have pulled the old-lady card and left. But I didn't have a clue. I found a seat on the sofa just as a goddess with red and gold curls floated into the room. I couldn't take my eyes off her hair. Untamed flames. Joan of Arc.

"I'm Harmony." She sat, folding her legs underneath her as though they were wings.

We introduced ourselves and my body relaxed a little as Harmony shared some of burlesque's fascinating past. History comforted me. I loved the fact that burlesque ridiculed lofty, uptight social mores. That it was about women making fun of the establishment. Satire I could do.

I'd been to Catholic school, after all. These women were trailblazers. Heroes. Willing to sacrifice reputation for enlightenment.

"This is going to be so much fun," Harmony said. "And you don't need to decide on your solos for a few weeks yet."

Solos? That was when I learned that our classes would culminate in a performance onstage in front of a real live paying audience. And during this performance we would be removing our clothes. When would I learn to pay attention to the fine print before signing up for things?

I was as oblivious to the future repercussions of that one tiny action – *sign up here* – as Jesus seems to be in this cathedral in Lugo. Gazing demurely down at me, he is altogether unaware of the crucifixion arrangements going on above his head. High above the marble pillars, naked cherubs float amidst silver clouds. A bare-chested angel, with an impressive six-pack, and wings like the Exterminating Angel in Comillas, raises the cross.

You couldn't just be ordinary could you? I want to whisper. *And now it's too late. Look away all you like, but your crown of consequences will find you.* Of course, it's not only Jesus I'm speaking to.

Despite the years of religious instruction at Catholic school – or possibly because of them – I never thought of Jesus as a human being. Flesh and blood. Like me. But I feel a new connection with this pole dancing messiah. I want to put my hand on his chunky chest, lean into him and whisper, *you look fabulous.* It seems somehow important that he knows he is beautiful. Even if he is doomed. But that would mean crossing the altar threshold and I'm not yet ready to commit that kind of sacrilege.

I say *Amen* and head into the bright Galician sunshine, on my own again for the first time in ten days. San Roman da Retorta is only a few short hours away. I stretch my ankle tentatively. Only a small twinge. The bus ride must have been good for it. The two apples and bottle of water in Petunia's side pockets should be more than sufficient to get me to the albergue.

I have not, however, factored in my poor sense of direction and inability to pay attention to the rules. Nor have I taken into consideration the possibility of encountering burlesque cows, Galician vipers or the black wolf.

11

The old town of Lugo is the start of the second stage of the Camino Primitivo. A sign tells me that the bridge I'm about to cross is a World Heritage site. The silver-bodied centurion guarding it is mesmerising. His legs seem flimsy and fragile, like tubes of tin foil. And when I touch him, he's curiously cool for being so shiny and it being such a hot day.

I run my hands along his metallic tunic, up his neck, along the bridge of his glittery nose. He has the chiseled Romanesque features and strong jaw one would expect of a centurion. His molten eyes draw me closer. Magnets. I peer into them, then pull back, scalded. It's the same expression that baffled me as a nine-year-old. And many years later too, in a park in Vancouver.

My discovery of the Kama Sutra, at age nine, was accidental. Amy was new to the school. A red-head with academic parents, she invited me home one day to her double-storey house. I had only ever lived in a single storey, and I'd always wondered what mysteries existed on second floors. She must have seen me gaze longingly at the stairs, because right after our cheese-and-tomato sandwiches, that's where we went.

I took my time up the winding staircase, touching the wooden banister with reverence, in hopes of somehow being transformed into an otherworldly creature. Or at least someone more interesting than my fourth-grade self. The room at the top did not disappoint. Its sharply-angled roof and tiny attic windows lit up the floor-to-ceiling bookshelves in slivers of light. I imagined that if I found just the right spot, a secret door would open, and Narnia would be revealed. But what transpired was in fact much more exciting.

Amy stood on her tippy toes as she slid a very large book off the top shelf. I thought it might be the Bible, it was that grand. Its thick brown cover looked like some kind of animal had died in the making of it. Amy motioned to me in silence to join her in a patch of sunlight on the orange shag carpet. She opened the book, giggling.

Flowery writing was scattered between the images, but it wasn't in any language I'd seen before. Anyway, I was more focused on the pictures of the very naked people. I twisted my neck trying to understand what was happening.

"It's sex," Amy whispered.

Sex! No one in my family had ever said that word out loud. I suspected my parents didn't even think it quietly in their heads. Certainly not my mother.

Amy and I spent the afternoon in the attic turning the pages as quietly as possible. Being not-yet-ten, all I knew about sex was that it was something you didn't talk about. Probably because it was common.

But the people in the pictures seemed to be having fun, even though they weren't wearing any clothes. And all the rooms were so pretty. One of them was like a little stage, with a huge golden bed framed with velvet drapes – exactly the same as the curtains in the Opera House! A lady with long curly hair, like snakes, was lying in the middle of the bed, on top of a man. They both had strings of pearls around their necks. He was staring into her eyes as though he'd found the Holy Spirit there. None of the adults I knew looked at each other like that. What happened when someone looked at you like that? Was *that* sex?

The chiseled centurion on the Heritage wall isn't only a reminder of my discovery in Amy's attic. He also makes me recall the Adam affair, something I don't want to do right now. So I cross the bridge, leaving him behind.

It's less than twenty kilometres to San Román da Retorta, but the Primitivo is an inland route and it's hot. I'm already missing del Norte's sea breeze. Because I have spent the last ten days blindly following Sylvia and Nico, I have not paid close attention to the little shells directing pilgrim traffic. But it's not that far to San Román. How lost can I get? Besides, Alfonso II did it without any arrows, or even roads, more than a thousand years ago. I can do this.

The first scallop marker is next to a concrete bridge on the outskirts of Lugo. Painted on a rock, it's faded and seems to be directing me to the gravel path next to the bridge. It's more of a trail than a road, whereas the alternative route, the one I'm on, seems well-travelled and friendly. But perhaps that's the point – the road less travelled, as the saying goes. It seems the option that Alfonso the Chaste would have chosen, austere and punishing. So I follow it.

The path gets narrower and narrower. This is a new kind of heat. As I reach into Petunia's side pocket for my water bottle, a cow meanders around the corner, her tail swishing from side to side. And then another. And another. There must be at least thirty or forty of the black and white beasts. All with the same rhythmical gait, they move in sync with one another, a bovine ballet.

The road is so constricted that there is nowhere for me to go. All I can do is stand still and hope that they are friendly. One by one they pass, glancing sideways at me, batting their long lashes. Even these Camino cows are sexier than I'll ever be.

Burlesque did not come naturally to me. Awkward and stiff, I could not strut. Or rotate my hips. And the idea of making a production out of getting undressed was about as shameless as taking change from the collection basket during mass.

The studio mirrors reflected seven fantastically fluid dancers – and me. Removing articles of clothing in time to the music, without falling over, was a challenge. Being seductive and confident while you did so, was near impossible.

But even though I was hopeless, I eagerly anticipated my weekly bridge crossing. It was because of the girls. All young enough to be my own children, they never made me feel old. My lack of skill had nothing to do with my age. It was the by-product of being Lindy-Lou, made rigid by aspirations of saintliness and years of ballet.

But I persevered. *That* I could do. I was inspired by Harmony's tales of renegade women through the ages, thumbing their noses at society, and at the men who thought they owned them, by getting naked. And who knew there were so many ways to peel gloves and stockings? I had never worn either, so putting them on was almost as complicated as taking them off.

"You look the audience in the eye," said Harmony, demonstrating a glove peel one evening while we watched her from the overstuffed sofa. This was the first studio I'd ever been in that had a sofa. In burlesque, I found out, the audience is as crucial to the performance as the dancer. The magic lay in their interactions. Genius! Except I had no idea how to interact.

"Pretend that you have the most fantastic secret," Harmony continued, biting down on one gloved fingertip, peeking coyly at us from under her lashes. "Let the audience know that if they give you their full attention, and adore you with all their might, maybe, just maybe, you'll share your precious secret with them."

I loved Harmony. And I wanted to please her, but I had a hunch my husband was right: seduction was just not in my DNA.

It takes forever for the cows to pass. Where are their people? Do they know where they're going? When the last one eventually saunters by, flicking her tail against my arm, I squat between the piles of poo and gulp at my bottle of water. How hot *is* it today? How long have I been walking? Why have I not yet seen another yellow scallop? Have I just not been paying attention?

Out of the corner of my eye, I notice a dark shape on a rock slightly behind my right shoulder. I freeze, mid-gulp, squinting my eyes. *Holy crap.* It's the black wolf! Just like the one the old man told his grandson not to feed. It can't be a wolf, can it?

Whatever it is, it has not eaten in a while. It's all ribs and spinal column. Like del Norte Jesus. Maybe it will ignore me, like the cows, if I don't move. But the throaty growl sounds like trouble. I stand as slowly as possible, willing it to go away. The rumble grows louder. And then everything happens quickly.

The air rustles and something compels me to take a swift sidestep, just as jaws bite down into Petunia. *Don't make eye contact.* I roar like a bear and hurl my water bottle at the beast. In some kind of miracle, the bottle hits his scrawny body and ricochets into the bushes. He chases after it, and I run in the opposite direction. When I stop running, I'm on a rocky path ascending a mountain. Lost.

A sea of boulders surrounds me. Not a speck of colour. One lone black tree is split in two like a sentry caught by surprise, unable to defend himself from attack. Or God's wrath. Even the sky is washed out. Grey. And I have not seen a scallop shell since that first one at the bridge. How long ago *was* that?

Every step threatens to dislodge an avalanche of rocks. The dirt trail disappears. No one has been here in a very long time. Possibly ever. Alfonso the Chaste surely did not come this way. Not without fancy hiking shoes. Where am I? Where is the rest of Spain? Sylvia said there would be no mountain today. This is definitely a mountain. And my ankle is pulsing angrily.

I lean against a rock, cursing myself for not considering the possibility of disaster. Not a fearful person, I tend to be pathologically naive in my assumption that things will turn out okay. I lack the gene that worries about long-term consequences. Until it's too late. Like taking off my clothes onstage. Or climbing into a camper van with a man I've just met on a street corner.

12

A few weeks after my mammogram, the lady from the office called. "May I speak to Lindy-Lou?" While nobody but my mother and my sister called me that anymore, it was still the name on all my official documents.

"That's me," I replied, thinking, *but is it?*

They'd found 'something' in my left breast, she said. They needed to do a biopsy, just to make sure that the 'something' they'd found was, in fact, nothing. She didn't make a fuss, so I wasn't worried. It sounded like a treasure hunt. Like maybe my left breast was hiding Hershey's kisses or a misplaced winning lottery ticket.

It was only the following week, with a needle poised above me, that I felt a pang of anxiety. And then only because the woman maneuvering the needle mentioned the word malignant – something I had not considered until that very moment. But it was over quickly. And no-one called me sweetie, which was lovely. There was a lot of Lindy-Lou-ing though, and I couldn't decide how I felt about that. I needed coffee to clear my head. Malignant was not an option. I had an unfulfilled destiny waiting for me. Maybe *that's* what was hiding in my boob.

On my way into Starbucks, a man with dreadlocks and see-through eyes smiled at me. "How's your day going?"

"Really well, thank-you." I apologised to God for the white lie, but I didn't think this clear-eyed stranger wanted to hear my truth right now.

"My name is Satya," he said.

"Lindy," I responded. *Just Lindy.*

There was a gap between his front teeth. And one corner of his mouth turned up every now and then, as if he was laughing at an inside joke. He talked for a very long time, and I was happy to stand there in the sunlight, my left breast still intact, watching him. He told me he had identified the seven truths to enlightenment. Why seven? Why not eight or ten?

"I can help you fix your life," he said.

Was I so obviously broken?

And then he told me he lived in a van.

"Does it have daisies on it?"

"You can see for yourself," he said. "It's parked at the beach right over there."

"You sleep on the beach?" Wasn't there a law against that?

"I sure do, with that view, and no taxes."

I was impressed.

"Wanna see my van?" he asked.

Of course I did. He was living my dream. Freedom. As we walked, he continued with his story. His journey to enlightenment was clearly not a short one.

The van was an upsetting beige-brown colour. No daisies. He opened the sliding door. I peeked inside. An old-fashioned white teapot rested on a cooktop. Next to it were two mugs – one black, one white – upside down on a neatly folded dishcloth.

Lined up on a shelf above the mattress at the back of the van, was a dynasty of white candles. On one end of the shelf was a framed black and white photo. Propped beside it was an atlas. It was old, like the one I had been thumbing through at home recently, the one I could not bring myself to give away, even though it was so old that South Africa was still divided into only four provinces. The atlas was a reminder of the fickleness of boundaries and the cruelty man is capable of inflicting on his fellow man to maintain the illusion of ownership. I always thought it admirable when someone did not succumb to that kind of perspective. Satya, with his disdain for bylaws, was clearly one of those people. I wanted to be like him. I made a mental note to get rid of some stuff when I got home. Maybe the atlas.

Satya climbed into the van and, in a remarkably graceful combination of movements, sat himself cross-legged on a large cushion behind the driver's seat. He patted a space beside him and I assumed that meant I should join him, so I did.

As my eyes adjusted to the dim light, I saw that the black and white photo on the shelf next to the atlas was of a female sitting on a tree stump. Naked and voluptuous. Her head had been cut off.

"Wow," I gushed, trying not to think of the headless woman. "It's so neat." Could I live like this? I am not very tidy.

Satya was in the middle of explaining how the stovetop worked when he stared at me. Like a hungry dog waiting to be fed. Maybe this was the Zen way. He took hold of my fingers and I noticed how very large his hand was. I waited for his words of wisdom. How lucky to have met Satya today! He would show me, if not the whole path, at least the first steps to finding my Way in the world.

My hand in his felt comforting. Like the time the vet had consoled me when he'd euthanised our fifteen-year-old cat. Before perimenopause, I'd only ever cried when I heard the national anthem. So I surprised myself that day, when tears popped out my eyes as the cat breathed her last sigh. The vet had held my hand just like this and patted my back to make me feel better. I expected Satya to pat my back, but instead he leaned into my neck and said, "You smell good."

Was his voice always this deep? I felt like Little Red Riding Hood, even though I was wearing purple tie-dye. Granny was dead, gobbled up, and here I was, happily holding the wolf's hand.

I was very proud of what I did next. I did not say "thank-you." Instead, I said, "I'm sorry," retrieved my hand, climbed out of the van and walked back to Starbucks.

"You'll never attain enlightenment," he shouted. "You're stuck in your bourgeois life of privilege. You'll always be broken."

I couldn't answer him because he was right. I had had such great plans for my life, and all I was, was a housewife in the suburbs with a husband who provided for my every need. And I was ungrateful. A tear trickled down one cheek. I hoped it was simply a delayed reaction to the needle in my boob. Or the headless woman in the van. Satya did not deserve my tears.

The sun has moved lower in the Spanish sky while I've been leaning against the rock, waiting for my ankle to stop throbbing, considering the options. It's been twelve hours since I left my little pilgrim family in Llanes, but it feels like days. My apples and water bottle are gone. Closing my eyes, I try to focus on the sounds. Nothing. *Nothing?* I'll have to keep moving – get to the top of the mountain. From the top, I'll be able to see roads or houses or people. Or at least, *please Jesus*, a Camino shell.

When I open my eyes, Satan is staring at my hiking boots. *Oh God!* I should have bought the muted old-lady shoes instead of these neon orange ones. They would have been far better for camouflage. The serpent's tail is curled into a tight hook, right beside his evil eyes, so it's hard to tell how big he is. But according to Sylvia's guidebook, size doesn't mean anything if you're a snake.

Can he see my pounding ankle? Sense my weakness? Will there be a warning hiss before he attacks? Will it be a slow and agonizing death? Or swift and sweet? There's no turning back now. The only way to get to the top of the mountain is to scale this venomous viper. Sylvia said snakes only attack when they feel threatened. How do I jump over him without scaring the living daylights out of him? Because I can't die today. Not one person on the planet knows where I am right now – including me. My body will never be found. My family will think I ran away from home.

Hail Mary, full of grace, the Lord is with thee. Mary is my go-to when I feel God might be a bit judgy. Mary knows how hard it is to be a good wife and mother. Burlesque Mary in Comillas, with her neon lights and flouncy stone skirt – she'd understand. So it's to her I pray. *Blessed art thou amongst women.* I bend my shaking knees in preparation and hope I can leap over his mottled head before he strikes. *Pray for us sinners, now and at the hour of our death.* His eyes flicker. I jump. *Amen.*

I move as fast as I can, which is not very fast at all. My fat ankle is slowing me down and I keep dislodging rocks.

If the snake *is* following me, perhaps the rolling debris will injure or frighten him.

The sun is disappearing behind the mountain. I keep panic at bay by telling myself that the Way will be visible soon. Fourteen hours after leaving Llanes, I reach the top of the mountain. I turn slowly, circling myself. There is nothing. No rooftops, no sounds, no windmills, no birds. I can't even see the path I've just come up on. I'm in trouble.

My fingers are swollen sausages, my wedding ring virtually invisible. The skin on my thighs droops across my kneecaps in paper-thin folds of dehydration, as though I am melting. As if at any moment my flesh will start dripping onto the rocks, leaving my skeleton exposed. Goosebumps rush across my body. My ears tingle. I'm so thirsty. And so unprepared for this pilgrimage.

The shaking starts. I am lost. In so many ways.

Surrender seems such a cowardly thing. Bargaining gives the illusion of power. And I have bargained many times in the past. With family. With God. Bargaining is part courage, part sacrifice. An eye for an eye. A trade between equals. But there are moments when we have nothing left with which to bargain. On our knees, annihilated, the only hope is that something bigger will lift us up. That it will carry us, bit by shattered bit, to where we, by ourselves, are unable to go. And that it will then rearrange us into a mosaic of splinters, reminding us that we are both nothing and everything.

I open my arms wide, like wings, look up to the sky – to God if he is there – and surrender. A loud white buzzing fills my head. As though bees have taken up residence in my skull. Without my brain to complicate matters, my body takes over, propelled by an unseen force. Maybe God. Maybe not. My lungs fill. And I run. Down. Down. Down.

13

I don't recognise anything. But my legs keep going, the fire in my ankle somehow fueling my run. The dirt road flattens and white butterflies, gleaming in the twilight, pull me along. I almost expect the Avenging Angel to swoop across the darkening skyline. But that would be ridiculous. He's hundreds of kilometres away, in Comillas, with neon Mary.

The sun disappears and the butterflies glow more brightly. Are they fluorescent? Or is this the white light of death? I turn away. And see the fountain. My legs buckle and Petunia and I land in a puddle of cow poop. I crawl towards the water.

The fountain is part of a stone pool, surrounded by long grasses. A face peers up at me from the water. A ghoul! On my knees, I gape below the surface. The ghoul is me, with black holes instead of eyes, cheekbones protruding, lips cracked. *Jesus.* I gulp from the pool and then, on my back, legs outstretched, I watch the first stars pop into the sky. This would be a good place to die. But not yet. I would be a hideous corpse right now.

The bees quieten. I roll my head slowly to one side. And there it is. A scallop shell on a stone marker. Underneath it is a yellow arrow. *Thank-you Mary!*

As twilight turns to pitch, I stumble into a crescent of trees protecting a fairy tale house lit by strings of twinkling lights. San Román da Retorta! Like a beacon of hope, a bald man stands in the doorway.

"Hola," he says, his smile flickering as I walk through the entrance. Without asking me to sign in, he guides me up the stairs to a room with four bunks and gives me the water bottle he's holding.

"Gracias," I whisper.

In the shower, I wash away the dirt, the sweat and near-death, recalling my daughter's parting advice. Just days before I left for Spain, she had patted my hand, and said, rather seriously, "Remember mom, stopping doesn't mean you've failed." *Oh?* "No one will know if you don't walk." She smiled at me as if I was the child and she the parent. "You can spend the next three weeks in spas, getting mani-pedis and massages." I got palpitations considering the consequences of a grand deception like that.

Too tired to contemplate tomorrow, I hobble towards the bunk nearest the window and pass out.

When I wake up, I'm disoriented. Then relieved. I'm in San Román da Retorta. Alive! I recite "Our Father" in my head, grateful for another day, then peek into the sleeping bag. Ribs. Hipbones. And wrists, disproportionately large. Knees, too, seem bigger than thighs. But the paper thin folds above my knees have gone, replaced with regular human skin. Thanks to water. And sleep. What a miraculous thing, this human body.

On that mountaintop yesterday, I was for a time convinced it would be my last day alive. That I would, in fact, be dead by daybreak. There was simply no way I could imagine finding my way back, I was that deeply lost. I'm still not sure how I got down the mountain, found the scallop, the albergue. There is no logic to the sequence of events. Was it God? Muscle memory? The butterflies? Pure dumb luck? And does it really matter? I am alive. And so is hope: if I could find *the* Way, perhaps I can find *my* way too.

In some inexplicable way, that's what burlesque gave me too – hope.

Walking stiffly onstage to the toll of bells the night I became Luna, I was thankful for the spotlight. It meant I couldn't see the audience. The gloves were the first to go. My fingers trembled. So did my kneecaps. Fear flurried through my ribcage as I unzipped my daughter's little black dress. There was a pounding in my throat. Was I having a heart attack? What if I died onstage? Half-naked? No one knew my real name. Who would tell my family? What would my husband make of the pasties when he was summoned to the morgue to identify me?

The music was not waiting for my panic to subside. There were stockings to be shed. As they fell to the stage floor I realised – much too late – that I was about to expose my gravity-ravaged bottom to a theatre full of strangers.

Turning my back towards the audience, I ran my hands down my forty-seven-year-old derrière, a gesture born of panic and a last-ditch attempt at modesty. The crowd reacted. Wildly. And just like that, my terror disappeared. Oh, my hands were still shaking. My legs still jelly. But I had not felt a thrill like this – ever. And that's when it happened – the little serpent hibernating in my coccyx uncoiled itself and shot through my central nervous system filling me with a kind of energy that I had not felt since my fifteen-year-old self skipped past the convent's blooming bougainvillea after confessing to Father Ignatius.

I had chosen the name Luna Blue because I assumed burlesque would be a once-in-a-blue-moon thing. I wasn't *that* kind of person. Someone who wears stilettos and false eyelashes and very tight dresses. Common.

But that first night, the audience so loudly appreciative of my uncoordinated middle-aged moves, something unexpected happened. Burlesque woke me up. In a startling way. I loved it! And suddenly the nature of my dilemma changed. As long as fear was what I was experiencing, I could convince myself that I was doing burlesque for all sorts of lofty reasons: to conquer my Catholic hang-ups and prudish upbringing and to protest society's uptight views on how women should dress and behave. But if I was enjoying it, then I couldn't be the good girl I'd been pretending to be for nearly half a century.

Lindy-Lou would never get undressed in front of two hundred strangers. Why, she would blush at the mere thought of doing something so scandalous. No, *she* would be home, cooking dinner for her family, watching TV with them after loading the dishwasher. But here I was, behaving like a shameless hussy. And relishing it! If I was not the virtuous person I always thought I was, who, in the name of all that is holy, was I?

It is this question that I carry with me on the Camino. I limp to the bathroom. Maybe I could just stay here in San Roman. I don't want to leave. What if I get lost again? Maybe I am too old, too clueless to do this. Maybe being a pilgrim will be just another unfulfilled dream. For the first time since arriving in Spain, I seriously consider what my daughter said about stopping.

The benefit of not going to Catholic school means that her decisions are unencumbered by fear of God or the possibility of spending eternity in Hell. She is wiser than I will ever be. Even her response to Luna Blue was pragmatic.

We were on the Upper Levels highway in the mini-van. I was the passenger, she the invincible new driver. I had told her about burlesque classes and she had agreed to lend me her black dress from Aritzia for my widow performance. I had, after all, paid an arm and a leg for it.

"You know mom," she said, changing lanes without signaling, "most people, when they have a midlife crisis, don't they just buy a fancy car?"

"Indicators!" I hyperventilated.

"Nick's dad got that black Porsche. And remember Sue's mom? She drives a really cool Harley now." She tucked a strand of hair behind her ear. "Why don't you just get a convertible or something?"

I couldn't answer. My mind was a soup of sweaty fear waiting for the inevitable collision. She adjusted the rearview mirror for a better view of herself, nearly rear-ending the Volvo in front of us. "So, now if my friends ask me what you do, do I tell them you're a stripper?"

My right foot desperately pumped the imaginary brake in the passenger seat.

"That's *so* not West Van. Having a stripper mom," she said. "But it's okay." She ignored the tight scream escaping from my lips. "If it makes you happy, you should do it."

It was only hours later, once my jaw unclenched and my head stopped pounding, that I realised she'd mentioned my midlife crisis as casually as Sunday brunch. And I thought I'd being doing such a splendid job pretending it didn't exist.

14

I brush my teeth, examining myself in the mirror in San Román. Surely a near-death experience should leave its mark? But I see nothing different.

The smell of coffee teases me out of the bathroom. I pack Petunia, roll my sleeping bag and grab my orange shoes from where I left them in the hallway. I down two cups of café con leche, pleased that there is no one else around. What must the other pilgrims have thought of me when I arrived last night, half dead and delirious? I tighten my laces gingerly and grab a banana. Delaying my walk is not going to make it any easier.

The landscape is soupy. How am I going to find my way in this fog? I hear voices and want to shout, "Wait up!" but that would be so needy. Instead, I hobble-run towards the sounds of conversation. Three young boys with backpacks are leaning against a tree. *Damn!* I'll have to keep walking.

"Hola," I say, passing them, rotating my leg slightly to relieve some of the pressure in my tendon.

"Buen Camino," they reply in unison. Is that pot I smell? Isn't that breaking some kind of peregrino rule? Maybe they're not pilgrims at all! Oh God, maybe I'm going the wrong way again. Where are the scallops? The arrows?

When I can no longer hear their voices, I crumple against a tree. Leaning against the trunk, I grab the banana from Petunia's pocket. Maybe I'm not cut out for this pilgrimage thing. I have been one half of a couple for so many years, and for almost as long I have wanted nothing more than to be a whole, all by myself again. To make my own way through the world. But I'm failing miserably. I couldn't even walk a few kilometres on my own yesterday without nearly ending up dead.

"Hola!" I hear through the haze, and see the boys walking towards me. How long have I been sitting here feeling sorry for myself?

"Hola." I fold the banana peel before popping it back inside Petunia, as though I have everything under control.

They wander past me, chatting away in Spanish. Do their parents know what they're up to? I grab onto the tree, haul myself up and follow them into the mist. Even if this isn't the right route, at least I won't be alone. Thankfully they're speaking so loudly that I can keep a respectable distance. It would be most unfortunate to be thought an old-lady stalker on a pilgrimage.

The fog lifts as we leave the trees, revealing a yellow scallop on a blue ceramic tile, set in a concrete marker – like a little police officer on the side of the road. Written underneath the scallop is one word: smile. So I do. Then the realization: the boys are heading in the direction of the rays! They're not walking towards the body of the sun, as I was doing yesterday! And from some dark corner of my brain, I recall Sylvia telling me that different regions of the Camino use the scallop shell differently. I nearly ended up an ugly corpse yesterday only because I was going in the opposite direction to where the scallop was directing me. I was obeying the incorrect rule, without knowing it.

The boys disappear. I lean into the concrete marker to stretch my Achilles one last time. Examining it more closely, I see that it isn't telling me to smile after all. What it says is '5 mile.' Five miles to where?

I've hated the number five ever since it killed my ballerina dreams.

I was fourteen, backstage at the Concours de Ballet, waiting for my number to be called. Names were never used in competition. We were only numbers. I was number five.

"Number three," the adjudicator announced.

Number three stepped confidently onstage, not a trace of nerves. I had been competing against number three for years, but still didn't know her name. This was not only because I was socially awkward. I was also intimidated by her talent. And, more recently, by her hiplessness.

When I turned thirteen, by some spectacular force of nature, I grew adult hips overnight. Number three still looked like a nine-year-old. Watching her from the wings, I felt more sadness than envy. It didn't matter how hard I worked, how much I sweated or starved myself, I would never again be hipless.

And then her music started. "Méditation" by Thaïs. *My* music. Dancers either had a pianist accompany them or their teachers provided recorded music. Number three had a pianist. I had a CD. My version of "Méditation" was in fact much more impressive than hers, since it was fully orchestrated. But this simply exacerbated our differences.

At least four inches shorter than me, number three was pure fairy. And she didn't seem to need to breathe. Which was extremely fortunate, since I don't think she could have fit human-sized lungs in her miniature torso. She made no noise as she pirouetted and jetéd across the stage. She may have floated for a bit, that's how light she was. When she finished, she drifted past me, applause ringing, not a drop of perspiration on her forehead.

I was not a floater. At the end of my performance I clunked my legs against the wall outside the stage door, sweat pooling under my hips. Staring at the swollen ankles above my head, I knew that my future, despite what my father had whispered in that darkened theatre a year earlier, would not include pointe shoes and tutus. Perhaps a habit would hide my hips?

When I had been searching for an idea for a burlesque solo, thirty-three years after this traumatic end to my dancing dreams, I had toyed with being a nun. I could still recite "Panis Angelicus" by heart, in Latin. I visualised a glorious un-robing to Andrea Bocelli's version. Instead of pasties, black duct tape crosses would camouflage my nipples. God would surely appreciate the gesture. But I couldn't find a habit that was easy to remove. And my daughter's tiny dress was perfect for the murderous widow choreography. It wasn't the size, so much as the construction, that made it suitable. The fabric was both stretchy and squeezy. And the long zipper gave me a fighting chance of actually getting it off.

The pièce de résistance was a scarlet corset that was revealed once the dress was fully removed. It took forever to get into the corset, and I only managed to lace it with help from the other dancers. Luna Blue was infinitely more patient than Lindy-Lou, who would never have spent so much time on her appearance. Since my hip growth-spurt, my wardrobe had consisted largely of baggy T-shirts and dungarees. So Luna Blue was a big surprise. The corset had given me, for the first time ever, a waist. Stilettos adorned me with elegance. False eyelashes completed the transformation.

I loved being Luna because she was completely unlike me. She was mysterious and interesting. Unencumbered by insecurities and regret, she was something my husband regularly told me I was *not* – fun. So when I was invited to perform my widow number again, just a few weeks after my burlesque 'graduation,' I didn't hesitate.

I had never been to the Waldorf. I wasn't even sure whether it was a theatre or a hotel. But two of the dancers from our graduating class had arranged the gig. It would be a reunion of sorts. I packed my toolbox, my trusty tombstone and my excitement in the mini-van and, after feeding my family, set off across the bridge. It was Monday night football. I would not be missed.

I pulled into the parking lot, relieved that I had not got lost. How was it possible that I'd lived in Vancouver for so long and there were so many parts I'd never seen? From the side entrance, it was a short walk along a dimly-lit passage to the dressing-room, where performers milled about in various stages of nakedness.

The exposed light bulbs around the mirror highlighted, rather unkindly, my age. It suddenly hit me: being a professional dancer was something my seven-year-old-self had longed for. Desperately. And now, all these years later, in the most unlikely way, that dream was being realised. I was being paid to dance. And I was nearly forty-eight years old.

When the stage manager poked her head around the dressing-room door, saying "Luna Blue," I felt suddenly light-headed.

"What about my tombstone?" I whispered into the back of her head as she led the way.

"Where do you want it?" she asked over her shoulder.

"It goes stage right, downstage." I knew all the lingo.

"Oh, there's no stage, hun." *No stage?* "Don't worry. I'll figure it out."

We stopped at the doorway, decorated with artificial flowers. *No stage?* I peeked inside. *Mother of God.* "It's a pub!"

"A tiki bar," she said proudly.

"And there are people, like, drinking and everything," I sputtered.

"Yeah, tiki bar." She marched onto the dance floor and placed my tombstone between a bunch of tables. How was I ever going to create the illusion of beauty and youth with the audience in spitting distance of my wrinkles and stretch marks?

I was contemplating a last-minute escape, when my music started. Out of options, I stepped through the plastic foliage. Avoiding eye contact, I removed my gloves, the little black dress and my lace stockings, all without hyperventilating.

Countless hours had gone into choreographing the next part of the dance, in order to preserve my dignity, because, of course, stripping is all about dignity. The night of my burlesque graduation, I had leaned over my murdered husband's tombstone, gazed mournfully at the audience, and slowly removed my old-fashioned movie-star bloomers. I had calculated the precise angle to ensure that when I finally revealed the scarlet G-string, my nether regions would be facing the black abyss of the wings. But on this night, in the Waldorf, where there should have been wings, there were instead floor-to-ceiling mirrors and cocktail-sipping tiki-patrons.

There was nothing I could do. No angle that would preserve my modesty. *It's just a bum,* I told myself. Perhaps Jesus would cause the gentlemen behind me to be distracted by their drinks, thus avoiding the scene about to unfold before their eyes. Exorcising the last remnants of Lindy-Lou from my frontal lobes, I poured my torso over the gravestone, effectively inviting every set of eyes in the bar to gawk at my raised bottom. Surrender. In all its glory.

As I removed the frilly bloomers, I was back in the garden of my childhood holding that little stick of fire. The burning sparkler moved closer and closer to my fingers. This time, I held on.

After the performance, I got dressed, collected my tombstone and loaded my belongings into the mini-van. As I drove away from the Waldorf, my legs felt longer, my backbone stronger.

It was nearly 2 am when the police officer flagged me down on Lion's Gate Bridge. Lindy-Lou would have panicked because that's what she did when she saw flashing blue lights. Luna Blue, however, was fearless. I had just exposed my middle-aged butt to a bar filled with strangers. There was *nothing* I couldn't do after that. I was also in the grips of a hot flush from Hell, so all the windows were open to let in the night breeze. This had transformed my heavily-sprayed burlesque up-do into a bird's nest of never-before-seen proportions.

The gracious officer ignored the false eyelashes drooping across my left eye and asked me whether there was any alcohol in my vehicle. I said there wasn't and he shone his flashlight into the mini-van searching, I suppose, for evidence to the contrary. What he found instead was a half-opened toolbox filled with pasties and glitter. And a tombstone on the backseat.

"Where have you been Ma'am?" he asked politely.

"The Waldorf." Luna Blue was unapologetic. "Dancing"

"Where are you heading now?"

"Home," I said brightly.

"Well, drive safely, Ma'am." He waved me along with his flashlight. I smiled all the way home, with a newfound respect for the law. And myself.

Burlesque was altering the very chemistry of my midlife self. For the first time, in a very long time, a kind of peace was settling into me. Driving back to sleepy Eagle Harbour did not feel quite as claustrophobic as it had for the past five years. Life in the suburbs as a nondescript housewife during the day might be workable if I could periodically try on this fearless alter-ego who was unruffled by police officers and gravity. It wasn't saving the universe, or creating world peace, but it was surely better than watching reality television. Wasn't it?

As I pulled into the driveway, I thought again about the sparkler. And how letting go was sometimes the only way to hold on. Or was it the other way round?

15

I can no longer hear the pot-smoking boys, but the stone markers on the side of the road give me a small sense of comfort. Yellow has never been my favourite colour, but these little yellow shells are making me very happy today. I hope my Achilles holds up, after the unintended extra distance I walked yesterday. It's thirty kilometres to Melide, my next stop, assuming I don't get lost again.

The fog lifts, the sun suddenly deadly and I am grateful for my bucket hat. Lightweight, with a wide brim, it has mesh windows for circulation, although the air is not moving today. The dirt track is flat, surrounded by acres of dry grass. No houses, no animals, no people. And not one cloud. Just relentless blueness. It reminds me of the walk to Güemes with Nico and Sylvia, the day I pulled my Achilles.

I miss my little pilgrim family. With them, there were no rules for who I should be. No assumptions, no expectations. On the Camino, we are all simply pilgrims.

We don't even have last names. Like Madonna. Or Sting. It's a kind of freedom. We wake up and we walk. That's all. And who we are when we walk, is who we are. No more. No less. Not unlike burlesque. It's why I miss Delilah too.

Delilah and I met at our first burlesque class, when I had no idea what I was getting myself into. She was twenty-one, almost six feet tall and her skin was so pale that it surprised me that the blood in her veins was not visible to the naked eye. Jet black curls cascaded down the length of her back. I could have stared at Delilah all day, she was that spectacular.

Three months after our graduating performance, the two of us were invited to perform at the opening of a new club downtown. Vancouver was home to a vibrant burlesque community and I was thrilled to be part of this parallel universe of glitter where no one called me Lindy. Not even Delilah used my real name, and I could no longer remember hers.

Delilah had promised to help me master the art of eyelashing. Like struts and hip rotations, false eyelashes were a conundrum to me. Sitting cross-legged on the sprung floor in front of the studio mirrors I felt more myself than I had in twenty years. Even though Luna Blue was the opposite of me in almost every way.

"What does your mum think about burlesque?" I asked Delilah as she gathered her hair in a ponytail.

"She thinks I'm doing yoga, and she's worried I'll go to Hell because it's not Christian."

Delilah's family had immigrated to Vancouver from Italy when she was two years old. One morning her father didn't wake up – dead of a heart attack at age forty-six.

Delilah lived in a duplex with her mother and paternal grandmother, both of whom still dressed in black, even though Delilah's father had been dead for five years. Church on Sundays was non-negotiable, as was weekly confession.

"What does your husband think about it?" she asked, squeezing glue onto the lashes.

"He thinks burlesque is like ballet but with different music."

"The way you do it, it kind of is," she giggled, attaching the lashes to her lids. In shared secrets, unlikely friendships are born.

My phone vibrated. My daughter was home alone, so I picked it up without checking caller ID.

"Hey gorgeous." *Adam!*

It had been ages since that day in the driveway. Luna Blue had not even been a twinkle in my toes then. This was unexpected.

"You there?" he tried again.

"Yes, I'm with a friend."

"OK, I'll be quick. Sorry I didn't call earlier. I was away on business and then vacation. But I'm back now. Can you do lunch next Wednesday?"

My brain froze.

"Hello?"

"Wednesday's fine," I said.

"Great! See you next week then." And he was gone.

"You okay?" Delilah asked. "You're almost as white as me."

"What does lunch with a married man mean?" I told her about the driveway.

"I don't think lunch means anything," Delilah said, sounding like my daughter. "You've got to eat, don't you?"

"Yes, I suppose I do."

"So, go eat."

I could eat. I could do this. I'd gotten myself into burlesque and was surviving just fine. It was only lunch, after all. Married people did lunch all the time.

"Thanks D." I kissed her beautiful pale cheek.

"You're welcome," she said. "Now, let's see this dance."

The show was in three days. I still didn't know how to do eyelashes.

Sweat trickles from my lashes, making my eyes sting. With no ocean nearby, the air on the Primitivo is a hot blanket. And then, in the middle of the nothingness, a Camino miracle: a stone shack with a board advertising ice cream. Petunia and I duck through the entrance. Hat off, I plunge my head into the deepfreeze. The man behind the counter glares at me. I pretend to examine the ice cream labels to buy more time in the cold air. When I sense his annoyance, I choose vanilla on a stick.

The man rings up my purchase on a till that appears to be as old as the Primitivo itself. On the counter, leaning against a display of toilet rolls, is Jesus in a box. He must be around two feet tall. A crown of thorns rests on his head. His beard is plastic, like the rest of him. But he has real hair, smooth and shiny. And very creepy. His hands are clasped in front of him in resignation, velvet sleeves hemmed with gold trim. In the middle of his burgundy robe is an elaborate sequin wreath circling a gold strawberry. The hem of his robe is embroidered with plump strawberries. At the top of each fruit, is a little tuft of berry hair with a cross peeking out of it. I don't remember learning about fruit in catechism class.

I'm so busy trying to figure out the Biblical significance of strawberries, that I almost don't see the Barbie doll. Much smaller than Jesus-in-a-box, she's wrapped in cellophane, and is propped on top of a three-pack of coconut soap. She's wearing a red mini skirt, floral blouse with puffy sleeves and red ballet pumps. I have never liked Barbie, with her tiny waist, her blemish-free skin, overarched feet and perfectly plastic life.

Until the night Delilah and I performed at the club.

My new dance was a throwback to the classics, Rod Stewart's version of "I Wish You Love." I had bought a long purple dress on sale in the old lady section at Sears. There was just enough bling on it to work, and it had long halter ribbons that I could untie easily while dancing.

I was briefly perplexed when the MC announced Luna Blue with her beautiful legs. *Beautiful legs?* I glanced at him just to make sure he knew it was me. He smiled, so I played along, seating myself on my prop for this number, a chair from home. It was part of a set – a dining table and six chairs from IKEA – our first family purchase after immigrating to Canada. The table was long gone, but I had kept the chairs and over the years they had been painted many different colours. This one was virginal white.

The stage was small, the audience close. As I wriggled out of my dress, a young woman reached out towards me. I didn't know who she was, but it didn't matter. Our fingers almost touching, she smiled and the translucent thread between us vibrated. The crowd went wild. A light inside me flickered. I felt like the teenager I'd never been.

I had invited a friend to the show. Jemma and I had known each other as students. She and her husband and children immigrated to Vancouver shortly after we did, and our families still regularly got together. She was the first person I welcomed into my burlesque world, because I knew she would tell me the truth.

"I was so worried," Jemma confessed when I caught up with her in the audience, after my performance.

"Why? You've seen naked women before." Jemma was a doctor.

"It's not that. I was afraid it wouldn't be you."

"What do you mean?"

"I thought you might be a completely different person up there to the person I know."

"But that's the point!" I almost shouted. "Up there I'm *not* me."

Jemma had known prudish Lindy-Lou who wore dungarees and hand-knitted sweaters, never did her hair or wore make-up. A virgin who barely showed her legs in public, certainly never her hips. That person didn't vaguely resemble Luna Blue.

"But you were still you. Authentic."

The word authentic always bothered me. It implied that you understood who you were and what you were doing. And I so clearly didn't. But Jemma's words made me rethink the role burlesque was playing in my messy life. I had thought it was allowing me to put on a different persona – a mask of make-believe. But I was beginning to realise that with each glove peeled, each stocking dropped, each layer stripped I was getting closer to my real self. A self I had never before met, or even suspected of existing.

"And that didn't disturb you?" I asked. "That it was *me* getting undressed?"

"No! I loved it!"

The young woman from the audience joined us. "That was so cool," she said, hugging me.

"Thank-you," I hugged her back.

"You look like Barbie," she added.

I hugged her harder. Six months earlier I would have been self-righteously offended at this comparison. But that night her words thrilled me. I had never felt this way before. Like a decoration. The angel on top of the Christmas tree. Was this how my sister had felt all her life?

Eyeing Spanish cellophane-wrapped Barbie in this stone shack in the middle of nowhere, with her teeny tiny mini skirt and red shoes, I wonder: did I only hate Barbie because I thought I could never *be* her?

16

Ice cream in hand, I walk towards Melide. The dirt becomes asphalt. It's hot and hard on my ankle. But it can't be that much further, so I walk faster. That way I'll be out of the sun sooner.

In three days, I will reach Santiago de Compostela. God will be waiting. He will be so proud of me for enduring, despite my dodgy ankle. For surviving the mountain, the snake, the lostness. God will tell me how to leave my husband, so that he can find a better wife, one who will not disappoint him.

Soon after starting burlesque classes, I did in fact tell my husband about the dancing. But he is not in the habit of asking clarifying questions and I chose not to elaborate. Lindy-Lou would have considered that lying by omission.

Luna Blue was less rigid about that sort of thing. In my defence, in the beginning I myself was not entirely aware of all the details.

Two weeks after my performance at the club, Jemma and her husband came over for a barbecue. They were on the deck, chatting to my husband. I was in the kitchen, making a salad. As I adjusted my Dollar Store glasses to inspect the mushrooms more closely, my husband filled the doorway, throwing me and the mushrooms into darkness. "What's it like being paid to take off your clothes?"

It was Sister Bernadette's *you think you're so perfect.* And just like that day in biology class, there was no right answer, because he wasn't really asking a question. That much I knew.

I lined up the mushrooms on the wooden chopping board. How could I explain that burlesque was saving me from spiraling completely into the Crazy? It would make no sense to him. It barely made sense to me. "Would you prefer I do it for free?" I asked, slicing the mushrooms very, very carefully.

He turned and walked away, still not noticing that I wasn't wearing my wedding ring. I had taken it off before my graduating performance, nine months earlier, and never put it back on. It was almost as liberating as I imagined chopping down the fence would be.

"Oops," Jemma apologised, taking his place in the doorway.

I had asked Jemma to record my performance at the club. I wanted to be sure that I didn't look completely ridiculous when I danced. Jemma had been so excited about it, that she'd just shown my husband the clip on her iPhone.

"I didn't know he didn't know."

"Oh, he knew," I sighed. "He just never asked for details. Can I see?"

I watched with squinty eyes, afraid of what I was going to see. There were parts of myself I'd never really *observed* before. I was still not a fan of my legs, but they were very different in heels. I got goosebumps listening to the audience. The whistles.

But I could not stop staring at Luna Blue's face. It was glowing, and it wasn't a hot flush. I searched for the wrinkles, the saggy jowls, the frown lines – but all I saw was happiness. This was nothing like the face that greeted me in the mirror every morning, the one with the lustreless eyes. This was who I wanted to be forever. But this was not the person my husband had married. The woman he'd promised to love, for better, for worse, was an unassuming housewife who wore tie-dye and Converse and cut her own hair. Not a common stripper with false eyelashes and a tarty hairdo.

The sign grabs my attention. *Albergue Alfonso II.* I have to sleep here tonight. I'm walking in Alfonso's footsteps after all.

The hospitalero takes me on a tour. The hostel is newly-built, he tells me. This is opening week, which explains why there are no other pilgrims. Anyone who actually planned their pilgrimage would not know about *Albergue Alfonso II's* existence. While I appreciate the shiny whiteness of the bathroom, with its modern plumbing and glossy tiles, I don't think Alfonso the Chaste would approve of the large pub overlooking the back garden.

I grab an almond chocolate bar from the vending machine and in the plastic silence of the covered deck, I page through the brochures stacked on the white tables. This is how I find out about the hundred virgins.

While young Alfonso was in exile, Mauregato, Alfonso I's illegitimate son, made a pact with the Muslim emir of Córdoba. King Mauregato promised to deliver one hundred virgins to the Muslims every year, in exchange for peace. When Alfonso II became king of Asturias, after Mauregato's death, he refused to send maidens to the emir. It was simply immoral, he maintained. Naturally, there were consequences.

The emir of Córdoba invaded the Kingdom of Asturias. But Alfonso retaliated, winning the Battle of Lutos, and killing the Moorish captain, Mugait. Henceforth, no virgins would be gifted to the Moors. What a legacy.

And yet, today, more than a thousand years later, there are still women being bartered, treated as disposable, less than human. And here I am, traipsing through Spain, pretending to be a pilgrim. Seeking a destiny as though I deserve one. Doing nothing about the many injustices perpetrated every day around the world. What would Alfonso think of me?

When the sun goes down, I am still the only pilgrim in Alfonso's albergue. I take my time reorganising Petunia and laying out my clothes for tomorrow. The bunks are grey metal, each bed with its own light. The side tables and cubicles are from IKEA. At one end of every navy-blue mattress is a fuzzy grey blanket and a pillow and sheet sealed in plastic. No sleeping bag tonight! For the first time since coming to Spain, I am alone in a bunk.

I climb into the perfectly creased bed, turn off the light at my head and think of Alfonso. Was he proud of what he did? Of the legacy he left? Of fulfilling his destiny? And what about his wife? How did she feel about their unconsummated marriage? Did she love him? Did he love her? Or did Alfonso's love also run wide, not deep? Was he a disappointing husband?

"I don't get it," my husband said, the morning after Jemma's barbecue reveal. He must have been stewing about Luna Blue all night. "Who the hell wants to see a naked forty-eight-year-old?"

I'd been asking myself the same thing. But in burlesque, in a peculiar turnabout, age is venerated, not covered in shame. It didn't matter that in real life I was old, uncoordinated and completely clueless regarding the art of seduction. Onstage, I became ageless, powerful and – miracle of miracles – beautiful. All of me. The wrinkles, the sagging body parts, the greying hair.

It was not the adulation of the audience though, that captivated me. It was waiting backstage in the sacred black silence. Something happened in the space between hearing my name in the darkness and stepping into the spotlight. I was seven again, waiting for the curtains to rise at the Opera House. And the connection between me and the audience was only a small reflection of what was occurring between me and myself.

I wanted my husband to understand why I loved this world of make-believe, and what performing meant to me. And so, eleven months after first stepping onstage as Luna Blue, I invited him to a performance. Of course, it was a horrible idea.

I left home around 6 pm. It was Saturday, hockey night in Canada, and if the game didn't go into overtime, the 9 o'clock showtime would work perfectly for my husband who would drive his truck over after the final whistle.

Delilah was in the dressing-room when I arrived, my IKEA chair in tow. As she lined her lips in black, I opened my toolbox to start the intricate process of becoming Luna.

"You okay?" she asked as I glued eyelashes. "What's up?"

"My husband's coming tonight." The lashes sagged across my eye.

"Why?"

"Because I invited him." I tried to remove the lashes but ripped them instead.

Delilah turned away from the mirror, waiting. What we both loved about burlesque was that when we performed we didn't belong to anyone. Onstage, Delilah was no longer the daughter of an overbearing mother and a dead father. She was just Delilah, the dancing Amazon with steel-grey eyes. And for longer than Delilah had been alive, my existence had been completely entwined with my family's. My youthful delusions of changing the world had been replaced with the realities of wifehood and motherhood. So being just Luna was liberating. Delilah knew all this.

"Why?" she asked again, insisting on the truth.

"Because he hates me doing this." I dug around in the toolbox for a tissue. I couldn't cry now. Tears would make an irreparable crack in the foundation and powder hiding my real face. I choked back the tears and found a spare set of lashes. "I'm hoping that if he comes he'll see the loveliness of everyone." I handed the new lashes to Delilah. "That burlesque isn't sinful."

"Keep your eye closed." She touched my forehead gently. "You know he's not going to change his mind."

I did know this. He had married me for my character. Because I was nice. He'd even said so once. Nice. Such a pathetic little word. But strippers weren't nice. They were common.

"Thank-you," I said to Delilah, as the lashes stuck.

She squeezed my arm then pulled her shirt over her head, revealing her perky boobs.

"I hope you appreciate those," I sighed.

"Oh, I do." She attached the black sequin pasties, turning first to one side then the other in front of the mirror to make sure she had angled them just right.

I zipped my long black bling dress with shoestring straps, another Sears purchase, just as a tiny brunette stuck her head around the corner. "You're up in five, Ms. Blue."

Oh God. Following her to the stage, I hoped that the hockey game had gone into overtime. That my husband was still watching grown men in helmets chase pucks around the ice.

I placed my black satin fingers on the white feathers draped across the chair onstage. I'd seen the boa on my way home from the library three weeks earlier. Displayed in the dance store window, amidst tulle and ribbons, it was on sale. My routine had been created around it. Each flick of the wrist and turn of the head had been carefully choreographed to perfectly match the lyrics of "My Way." The greatest irony was the song title: after forty-eight years on earth, I still had no idea what My Way was. Or any way, really.

Even through the too-bright spotlight, my husband was visible, leaning against the back wall. Towering above the other patrons, arms folded, his distaste floated above their heads and snaked itself around my throat.

Frank Sinatra started singing, and the flame in my solar plexus hissed, then fizzled out, turning my smile into a grimace. Even my teeth were cold. It was nothing like any of my previous performances, where the terror I felt as I stepped onstage was transformed by my connection with the strangers who cheered me on. My husband's judgement severed the bond of mutual adoration between me and the audience. I wanted to be angry. But sadness leaves space for nothing else.

I left the stage and got dressed. Delilah opened her arms. I stepped into them. The world, I think, can be divided into two kinds of people. Those who think that the right words, prettily spoken, can make things better. And those who understand that sometimes nothing is the only thing to say. Like my childhood friend Samantha, who never tried to make me feel better when Charlie died, but lay with me, watching clouds, sharing my sadness.

Delilah and I stood for a long time in the silence between two worlds, her chin resting on top of my head, her heart beating in my cheek. And then I had to go.

My husband walked me back to the mini-van, carrying our fifteen-year-old IKEA chair.

"So did you like it?" I asked as he closed the trunk.

"It was a good show," he said. I held my breath. "But I hated that my wife was in it." He sauntered off to his truck, parked in a side street.

The tears I'd swallowed earlier in the dressing room slipped out. It didn't matter anymore about the makeup. By the time I got home, my husband was asleep. I packed all my burlesque bits and pieces in the toolbox: pasties, hand-beaded G-strings, costume jewellery, hairspray, body glitter, false eyelashes and the only tube of lipstick I ever owned. Thigh-high stockings and the Audrey Hepburn gloves followed. Then safety pins and the double-sided carpet tape used to attach pasties to human flesh were added. There was no room for the scarlet corset, so it went into my sock drawer, along with the postcard advertising Luna Blue's debut performance a year earlier.

I pushed the toolbox as far back into the passage cupboard as it could go, behind six years of tax returns and the containers filled with seashells.

And just like that Luna Blue was dead.

17

The silence wakes me in the morning. No snoring! And what luxury to have a bathroom to myself. I savour the space and the quiet, before stepping outside.

While Alfonso's albergue is clean and modern, Melide itself is dilapidated and dirty. Garbage cans overflow and cigarette butts litter the pavement. I walk faster, trying to escape the grime, ignoring the ache in my ankle.

Did Alfonso walk this way? Did he walk alone? As the king he must surely have had an entourage. Would he have invited his wife to walk with him?

I haven't been walking that long, when I see a narrow entrance on the side of the road. *Ixrega de Santiago de Boente*, the sign above the doorway says. Inside is a tiny chocolate-coloured chapel with cream-coloured walls, a grown-up Kinder Surprise. A chandelier dangles from three gold chains above the altar. Four white candles poke haphazardly from the chandelier as if shoved there by a toddler having a tantrum.

The wall behind the altar is gold and lined with statues. On top, in the centre, is Saint James on his white horse. With no hands on the reins he is triumphant. The story of James' first miraculous appearance, when he had been dead for more than 800 years, is still fresh in my mind after reading about it last night.

King Alfonso II had died and King Ramiro I was in power. The Moors, growing afraid of the Christians' military strength, demanded the reinstatement of the gift of virgins. When King Ramiro refused, war was declared.

The Christians were defeated in the first battle and took refuge on Mount Clavijo. Saint James appeared to King Ramiro in a dream, promising him victory. The next day, fuelled by his dream, the King attacked. The Spanish soldiers, certain of defeat at the hands of the Moors, invoked his name "Sant Iago! Sant Iago!" Saint James descended from the heavens on his white horse, waving a banner bearing a blood red cross, just as depicted here on the wall in front of me. With his sword, he single-handedly slaughtered sixty thousand Muslims, leading the Christians to victory.

Since that day he has been known as Saint James the Moor-slayer. It is a very different Saint James to the one who wears a scallop shell bucket hat and carries a pilgrim staff. Which is the real Saint James, I wonder?

On the wall below Saint James on his stallion, is a red-robed man with a brass staff in one hand and a large book in the other. The Bible? Most certainly not the Kama Sutra. He wears a funny black hat and in front of him lies a golden sheep. Who *is* he? And why is he scowling at me as though I have disappointed him? Just like my husband.

There are voices in the chapel doorway. I stretch out my Achilles and glance at the man with the black hat one last time. I will have to find out who he is. Stepping through the tiny arched doorway, I almost collide with a pilgrim carrying the biggest backpack I have seen.

"Buen Camino," he says. His eyes are startling. They are the colour of the drop-waist wedding dress I wore nearly a quarter century ago. A kind of faded turquoise, it's not a common colour. Not for a wedding dress. Nor for eyes.

Distracted, I cross the road, and find myself surrounded by crumbling headstones.

The day after Luna died, I visited the cemetery in East Vancouver, not far from where I'd danced for the first time a year earlier. It was drizzling. A chipped tombstone caught my eye. It belonged to a father and three children, all dead on the same day. The epitaph was simple: *It is by dying that one awakens to eternal life.* Was it St. Francis who'd spoken these words?

I had read many biographies of saints during my time at Catholic school. Later on, I would read about Buddha with the same kind of zeal. And the Sufi mystics. And philosophers through the ages. The one thing they seemed to have in common was their ability to walk away from real life. Out the door they went one day, leaving behind their earthly responsibilities, their families, the drudgery of everyday existence. To live a Meaningful Life. Could I do the same? *Should* I do the same?

The drizzle in the cemetery thickened, forcing me to find shelter under a tree. A small grey square under my feet said *Sarah*. Below her name were the dates of her birth and death and three words: *Wife and Mother*. I burst into tears.

"I'm sorry for your loss," a voice said behind me. A man with crinkled skin was sitting cross-legged on the grass, leaning against the tree.

"I didn't know her," I sniffed, wiping my nose with the back of my hand.

He offered me a handkerchief. It was white, with an embroidered grey pinstripe edge.

"Oh, I can't use this." The only person I knew who used hankies was my father. And that had been thirty years ago.

"It's clean," he laughed.

"But I'm not. I'd ruin your hanky."

"I have more. I buy them in bulk at Costco."

I took it, grateful.

"If you didn't know her, why the tears?"

"She didn't accomplish anything. She had an unexceptional life. Never changed the world. She was just a wife and mother." I was not only talking about dead Sarah.

Since falling so unbecomingly into the Crazy, I'd crossed paths with some of the modern-day spiritual gurus who boldly proclaimed their five- or seven-step paths to enlightenment, abundance, fulfillment, happiness. I'd read their books, listened to their stories, observed wide-eyed their polished personas and fancy-filtered lives. And wondered why it eluded me. What kept me glued to the mediocre confines of my own ordinary existence? The tears resumed. *Damn perimenopause.*

"You want to sit down?"

I did. Next to him, on the slightly soggy ground, I hugged my knees towards my chest.

"You're a wife." He eyed my naked ring finger. I was still not wearing my wedding ring. And my husband had still not noticed. But decades of sun exposure while wearing it had left a faded band that was not so easy to erase.

I nodded, blowing my nose. His handkerchief would never be the same.

"Does your husband love you?"

"Yes."

"And do you love him?"

"Not enough," I said.

"What's enough?"

I didn't know. I rested my head on my knees and breathed the exhaustion of not knowing deeper into my veins. My body grew heavy. When I lifted my head again, the man was gone. Clutching his snotty embroidered hanky, I drove back across the bridge. To my husband. And children. The piles of laundry. And the fenced garden I never aspired to. The terracotta pots on the deck. The bills and dishes. Home.

The disintegrating headstones in Boente must be really old. I can't read any of the names. Even the dates are barely legible.

"You again!" It's the pilgrim with the gargantuan backpack. "I'm Tom. From Tasmania."

"Lindy." I shake his hand.

"You here on your own?"

I really should say no. "Yes."

"Where's your husband?" He eyes my wedding ring, back on my finger.

"At home."

"Where's home?"

Oh. My. God. Can't he see I'm wearing my do-not-speak-to-me face?

"Vancouver," I say, even though I suspect he's referring to my South African accent.

"But you're not Canadian," he says accusingly.

"I am now," I insist, feeling like a stubborn three-year-old. Does he not understand that I don't want company?

Somehow, he is beside me as we leave the collapsing graveyard. This is not how the Primitivo is meant to go. I left Nico and Sylvia so that I could walk alone. Besides, Tom feels like trouble. And I don't need any more trouble. I've had enough of that to last me a while.

A few weeks after I buried Luna Blue in the passage cupboard, I struck a pothole while maneuvering my shopping cart through the parking lot at Safeway. The bag of mandarin oranges perched on top, hit the ground and split open. Mandarins scuttled between the cars. Abandoning the cart in the middle of the road, I chased after them.

A motorcycle screeched around the corner, stopping a breath from my toes. The biker patted my trembling arm with his leather-clad hand, got off his bike and helped me gather the runaway fruit.

"Thank-you," I said, as he loaded the groceries into the van.

"You're welcome." With his hands free at last, he removed his helmet. *Thor in the suburbs.*

"I'm heading to Starbucks," I said, trying not to stare. "Can I get you a coffee?" It was the least I could do.

"Mighty kind of you Ma'am." *Ma'am?*

We sat at a table on the sidewalk with our Americanos. He was from Texas, a stuntman working on a movie being filmed in Vancouver. I think he said his name was Mike. But maybe it was Mark. I don't think he told me the name of the movie, but maybe he did. So much about him was distracting.

"Lovely colour," I said, staring at his motorcycle.

"Heron blue," he said, all eye crinkles and biceps. "You ever been on one?"

I shook my head. I was almost as afraid of motorcycles as I was of horses.

"Let's go then," he said.

Let's go?

"You bought me a drink. I owe you a ride. I've got a spare helmet."

His logic seemed somehow flawed, but he clearly recognised my ambivalence. He gave me the helmet. I put it on. He tightened the chinstrap. I climbed aboard.

"Hold on tight," he said, reaching back and pulling my stiff arms around his torso. His were definitely the kind of abs movies were made of. "Here we go!" I could hear the smile in his voice.

Oh God. All my identification was in the mini-van, along with the bruised fruit. If I met a fiery end on the Sea-to-Sky highway, or if my body was abandoned in the forest on the way to Squamish, hacked to pieces, no one would know it was me. Mike or Mark must have felt my heart hammering in my chest, because he reached back with one hand and patted my thigh. And then he left his hand there. I panicked. Steering a motorcycle with only one hand was surely not safe. *Relax! He's a stuntman.*

I had driven along this road countless times, but never like this. Sitting behind Mike on his heron blue motorcycle, everything seemed more dazzling. The ocean was brighter. The dandelions were happy little beacons on the side of the road. Above us eagles circled. Even the clouds were fluffier. And it wasn't just because of Mike's young hand on my middle-aged thigh. It was seeing the world in a wholly new way. I was part of the universe. *In* it, not merely an observer. Mike and I were disturbing the air with our presence. I was keenly aware of being close to the earth. To life. To death. This was power and freedom and bravery and beauty all wrapped up together. I did not want it to end.

"That was incredible," I said, as we pulled up to Starbucks again. My fingers were stiff from the cold, so Mike removed my helmet. "I didn't know you could smell the ocean from the highway." I hoped my nose wasn't running all over the place.

"Yeah, it's pretty special, getting around like this. Makes you really appreciate God's fine work," he said.

My heart warmed at this beautiful boy who spoke of God. "Thank-you for that." I hugged him. *And for keeping me alive.*

"Happy to be your virgin ride." I was thrilled he didn't say ma'am again. He lowered his visor and rode off, one hand raised. It would not have surprised me to see lightning shoot from his fingers.

18

It was only when I was back home, depositing the salvaged oranges in the fruit bowl in the kitchen, that I wondered what the hell I'd been thinking. If my teenage daughter ever pulled a stunt like that, I would ground her for life. What kind of mother behaved so irresponsibly? I unpacked the rest of the groceries, remorseful. My cheeks were still cold when the phone rang.

"You still game for lunch?" Adam. *Crap!*

I'd canceled our previous lunch arrangement – the one we'd made when Delilah and I were at the studio – to get my biopsy results. Just as I'd expected, there was nothing sinister going on in my boob. I was apparently a cysty kind of person. But my doctor still wanted to see me and the only available appointment was during the time Adam and I had scheduled lunch.

Adam wasn't too put out when I cancelled, which made me feel better about everything. Like it wasn't a big deal. I had clearly made a drama out of nothing. That had been months ago, when Luna Blue was still alive.

"Sure, when?" I asked Adam. I'd just been on the back of a motorcycle with a stuntman for God's sake! Of course I could do a silly lunch.

"Tomorrow?"

Oh. That soon. That was the tricky thing about lunch. There really was no excuse not to do it. As Delilah said, people have to eat.

"Sure." I could be cool about this. "Where should I meet you?"

"How about Stanley Park?"

I felt instantly better. Stanley Park meant fresh air and loads of people. Maybe we could even do a walk. Not too long. I wasn't much of a walker.

But of course, that's how the universe tricks you – it makes you think you've got everything under control and then throws a thunderstorm your way on a perfect blue-sky day.

I called Delilah immediately after my conversation with Adam. While we no longer danced together, we still kept in touch. She was a living memento of my short-lived bravery. Delilah had told me one day in the studio, that she was still a virgin, effectively shattering the myth of the slutty stripper. If my husband had been even vaguely interested in dismantling the burlesque stereotypes that lived in his head, I would have told him about Delilah. But he wasn't.

"How long has Adam been married?" Delilah asked.

"I don't know. He's younger than me."

"How much younger?"

"Five years? Ten years? Does it matter?"

"I suppose not. Not if it's just lunch."

"What do you mean *not if it's just lunch*?" I hyperventilated. "It *is* just lunch!"

"Maybe he's having marital problems." She sounded hopeful.

"Should I cancel?" I was so confused.

"No. Maybe he wants your advice. You know how people *love* to tell you stuff." I imagined her rolling her eyes. But she was right. For some reason, people did love to tell me stuff.

"We're meeting in Stanley Park," I added.

"Oh that's a good place to meet." Delilah sounded so confident that I forgot she had never been in a serious relationship. "You'll have a little walk. He'll talk. You'll grab a bite to eat. He'll feel better. You'll have done a good deed." That sounded just up my alley. I couldn't save mankind, but perhaps I could save Adam. I loved Delilah.

The next day I hopped in the mini-van, popped Leonard Cohen in the CD player and drove across the bridge. "Dance me to the End of Love" floated through the speakers. I'd once read an interview where Leonard explained that the lyrics had been inspired by the Holocaust. The Nazis had created orchestras at the concentration camps, composed of prisoners. These prisoner-musicians were forced to play as their fellow prisoners were taken to the gas chambers. What must it have been like – making music, watching your friends and family being marched to their death? Beauty and horror wrapped together so tightly. I tried to think of something less atrocious as I drove into Stanley Park, otherwise I would not be terribly fun company.

When I got there, Adam was waiting on a bench. Good Lord, he was beautiful! He was wearing jeans and a white golf shirt. When he smiled, his eyes crinkled, and I noticed a dimple in his chin I had not seen before. Beside him on the bench was a picnic basket. How clever of him! It was a lovely day for a picnic.

We found a spot under a tree, part sun, part shade. He spread a tartan blanket on the grass and opened the basket. It was filled with cheeses, pâtés, fancy cold cuts, crackers, cherries, chocolate and champagne. There was a wooden cheese board, silver cutlery and napkins. And two champagne glasses. Real ones.

I peered around nervously as he popped the cork. It was illegal to drink alcohol in public in Vancouver. But Adam did it so confidently. Brazenly. Was champagne exempt from the law? Like rich people?

I would have to drive back across the bridge later. What if I was stopped by the police? Failed a breathalyzer test? I could go to jail! My palms were sweaty. But Adam had made such an effort. Maybe I could have just one sip. We clinked glasses. *Oh.* Why had no one ever told me how delicious champagne is?

I sipped as Adam spread pâté on the crackers. I sipped as he arranged cherries and squares of Green & Black's chocolate on a shiny platter. I sipped while he chatted about his recent trip to Vegas. I sipped and sipped and sipped.

And then, all of a sudden, my head was spinning.

"I need a walk," I interrupted Adam mid-sentence. What had he been saying? Had he just told me he was unhappy? Did I miss my opportunity to help? I was *such* a bad person.

"Let's go then," he said brightly. He tossed the garbage in the bear-proof trash cans and wiped down the silverware. Very neatly. I had never seen a man do this before. He probably didn't leave his underwear lying all over the place. I suddenly wanted to see his sock drawer. He'd be horrified at the mess in my house.

We deposited the picnic basket in Adam's red convertible. It was the kind of red I liked, more tomato than strawberry, and it was so sparkly. Inside and out. The last time the mini-van was this clean was the day we'd bought it. Then Adam led the way to a path between the trees. It was so quiet. Not even our feet made crunching noises. This was The Magic Faraway Forest, not plain old Stanley Park in the middle of the week.

As my head started to clear I noticed the little stream running beside us, filled with rocks. Amongst all the grey and white, was one smooth black rock, the exact colour of the crystal next to my bed. Obsidian. I scooped it out of the water. As I lifted it up to the light filtering through the trees, Adam leaned into me.

"You're beautiful, you know," he said. I thought I had misheard him. "You have a beautiful face." He reached for my hand. He *did* say beautiful! Was he trying to make a fool out of me? My chest thumped wildly. His hand was impossibly soft. My skin had never been that smooth. Not even when I was twenty years younger. But his fingers, circling mine, puzzled me. What was I meant to do now?

I felt his eyes on me and glanced up. I recognised that expression! It was the one I had seen in Amy's attic when I was nine. It was the way the man on the fancy bed was looking at the lady who was lying on top of him. Like he'd discovered the Father, the Son and the Holy Ghost in her eyes. *Oh my God!* I was virtually having sex with another woman's husband in broad daylight. Was she home with the children, all dowdy? My mother and Aunty Bettie were *so* wrong. My scruffy jeans and tie-dye shirt had not saved me from being a tart. I would go to Hell for this.

I was suddenly tired. More tired even than the time I ate a whole bag of liquorice and passed out on the sofa in the middle of the afternoon. More tired than the day in the cemetery when the man with the handkerchief asked me what was enough. Even my ear lobes were tired.

I thanked Adam for the picnic, removed my hand and left, still clutching the little black rock. Leonard was singing

"Hallelujah" as I drove out of Stanley Park. A song about lust. And betrayal. And hurt. I wasn't sure whether I was crying because I was such a bad wife or because no-one had ever looked at me the way Adam just had.

I feel Tom's eyes on me, forcing a decision. We're at the albergue in Arzua, where I wanted to sleep tonight. But Tom is staying here, and there's something about Tom that's unsettling. So I tell him I will be continuing on, that I had planned on reaching O'Pedrouzo today. God will forgive the lie under the circumstances, I think.

"Good luck, Canada," he says. "Maybe I'll see you in Santiago."

I don't think so, Tasmanian Tom. I don't think so.

19

I had no idea what to do in the aftermath of lunch with Adam. An intervention was necessary. I asked my husband that evening whether his extended medical benefits covered therapy.

"Why?" he'd asked, eyes glued to a bunch of men in tights chasing a football. "What do you have to be unhappy about?"

He was right, of course. I had a husband who loved me, two healthy children, a house in the suburbs, a dog, a mini-van and a fence. I even had magnolia trees. How could I possibly be unhappy?

My husband unscrewed his Diet Pepsi as the cameras panned to the cheerleaders in their blue and white outfits, jumping up and down. I quelled the urge to shove the Pepsi down his throat and instead, did what any sane middle-aged woman would have done under similar circumstances: I found a psychic.

My first shock came when Victoria opened the door. With its stunning water views, her False Creek apartment was nothing like the Hansel-and-Gretel cottage I'd been expecting. And Victoria, glamorous in a white power suit, seemed more politician than fortune teller. Where were the flowing robes? The chunky crystal jewellery? Why did it make me sad that her hair was in a bun?

It was hard to know how old she was. Her face was unnaturally smooth, her inquisitive eyes framed with delicate lines, as if she were made of porcelain and could, at any moment, disintegrate right in front of me, if I said anything inappropriate.

"Have a seat, my darling." She sounded like the Queen.

I sat in the stiff white chair and handed her my cash.

She pushed my hand away gently, saying, "Oh no, keep that for now. Until we know if anyone's going to come through for you."

Come through? I was still contemplating what that meant, when she asked, "Who's Elizabeth?"

"My husband's mother." I was mystified.

"She adores you."

"Pardon me?"

"She's here," she said, as if it was of entirely no consequence that my mother-in-law had been dead for more than a decade. Victoria wasn't just a psychic. She was, she explained, a medium. She spoke to dead people.

I had wanted to tell Victoria about being a bad wife. All the things I had done. About the restlessness. Satya in the van. The stunt boy on the motorcycle. How Adam had made me feel when he looked in my eyes. And how much I missed Luna Blue. I wanted to ask her where my Big Life was hiding. I needed to confess, out loud, that there were days when I wondered what it would feel like to drive into the ocean. That I was afraid that that might be the only way to escape the chaos. The Crazy. But how could I do that when my mother-in-law was in the room?

So when Victoria asked me why I was there, I burst into tears. "I never wanted a fence."

"A fence?" she asked politely.

"Yes, a fence in the suburbs. And I have a grey mini-van." Its greyness seemed suddenly important.

Victoria handed me a tissue. This crying thing was really annoying.

"My … husband … says … I'm … ungrateful." It took forever to get the words out, I was crying so hard. "I'm … a … bad … wife." My husband had given me so much. "And I don't know what to do." I struggled to breathe. "I always thought I was a good person, but I'm not."

Victoria waited. Then she said, "Your father is here too."

Something inside me unplugged. More tears. I would never be able to speak again.

"Is there anything you'd like to ask him?"

There were so many things I wanted to ask my father. What was Heaven like? Did he miss me? Why didn't he tell me he was dying? But it was the most important question that popped out. "Is he disappointed in me?"

Victoria reached over, covering both my hands with her manicured fingers. "Your father loves you, my darling."

I watched her hands on mine through the tears.

"And you need to understand," she continued. "That where your father is, there is no judgement. You are the only one judging yourself."

I didn't believe it then. And I don't believe it now, leaving Arzua and Tom with his turquoise eyes. If I learned anything during catechism classes, it was that someday I will stand before God and be judged. And no amount of father or mother-in-law love will save me then.

I walk an extra twenty-two kilometres to escape Tom and his trouble, risking complete annihilation of my Achilles. On the plus side, though, I'm that much closer to Santiago de Compostela. And God.

On the outskirts of O'Pedrouzo, people in fancy clothes are milling about laughing outside a little white church. Leftovers of a wedding party. The bride and groom are nowhere in sight. I pass the stragglers, enter the church and walk up a narrow winding stone staircase, not sure if it's allowed. Four wooden benches overlook the red carpet running the entire length of the aisle below. White roses are attached to each pew with pink tulle bows.

Behind the altar, an enormous scallop shell fills the wall. Inside the shell is the messiah of my youth. Stoic. Uncomplaining. Nails are hammered through the bones of his hands and feet, and a crown of thorns rests on his head. He is bleeding for my sins.

Hands clasped in resignation, Jesus' martyred expression is the same one my mother wears when no one helps her in the kitchen. It's the look I have, with horror, seen on my own face in the rearview mirror, on more than one occasion. I want to shake Jesus and say: *You could have avoided this you know! You had strings you could have pulled. So don't go making me feel guilty.* Instead, I drop to my knees and whisper: *Our father, who art in Heaven.*

From a little door on one side of the altar a nun appears, dressed top-to-toe in white. She starts singing. "Panis Angelicus." It's Catholic school again, with all the promise of my teenage self. The pure intentions. The virtue. How did I go from *that* person to a woman who allowed married men to whisper sweet nothings into her pink neck in the middle of the day, an ungrateful wife who cried on strangers in cemeteries because she had a family who loved her?

When I left Victoria's waterfront apartment that day, she hugged me. "Remember, my darling," she said. "Just because things don't make sense, it doesn't mean they're not real." She felt airy.

I parked outside the first green Starbucks mermaid I spied. It was in a part of town I didn't know well. From my table overlooking Broadway, I tried to decipher Victoria's message while I scooped foam from my cup. There was so *much* that didn't make sense.

A woman with orange streaks in her grey curls parked a shopping cart outside the window. The streaks wriggled, like tiny worms in her head. Her cart was filled with bags, mostly the black garbage kind, except for the bright pink one on top. *Victoria's Secret*, it said, more glittery than a stripper's G-string. The woman removed a styrofoam container from the bag and got comfortable on the curb, her legs poking into the busy street.

From behind the safety of my overpriced coffee, I watched as she ate a burger from the styrofoam. Then she started pulling garbage bags out of the cart. She seemed distressed. I couldn't just sit there.

"What are you looking for?" I asked, joining her outside.

"The truth."

Why had I never thought to search for the truth in my shopping bags? She pulled things from the bags. There were shoes and books, an electric toothbrush, a navy vase with a white Gerbera daisy. A gorgeous lime-green retro toaster. Would it be rude to ask if I could buy it from her?

She stopped moving the bags about and squinted at me. Her eyes were green. Like mine. "What are *you* looking for?" she said.

The air stirred. The worms in her hair fidgeted. So did the little serpent in my coccyx.

"I suppose I'm also looking for the truth." If my husband could hear me now he'd pat my head and say, "Good luck finding anything but salmonella in those bags." He was like that, my husband. Practical. Sensible. It's what made him an outstanding provider. A reliable husband. A much-loved father. He was securely attached to reality. It was how I could afford to flit about and be all existential.

"I was meant to save the world," she said, so sadly that I had no choice but to hug her. Right there on Broadway, her little orange creepy-crawlies frolicking on my cheek, pedestrians waiting at the traffic lights, the chubby-cheeked barista watching us from behind his shiny window. She felt as airy as Victoria-the-medium. As insubstantial.

"I'll be seventy soon," she said, pulling away. "And I've saved no-one. Not even myself."

"It's never too late, is it?" My question was more for myself than for her.

Her expression suggested that I was the mad one. She went back to her bags, turning me invisible. For a moment, she rested her hand on *Victoria's Secret*, as if truth was indeed slumbering there, safely camouflaged by sequins.

I offered her the change from my coffee. She smiled, revealing a gap where there should have been front teeth. I didn't want to be rude, so instead of staring at her toothlessness I looked down. And that's when I noticed her shoes.

Red Converse. Like mine.

20

The nun in the clamshell chapel in O'Pedrouzo is no longer singing. My ankle twinges as I slide out of the pew. If my Achilles holds up, I will reach Saint James tomorrow. I will kneel in his cathedral and wait for my answers. I think of the bag lady on Broadway again. We are the same. But while my search is padded with privilege, hers is confined to shopping carts on busy streets. Is she my future if I don't pull myself together – towards myself? If I fail to control the Crazy?

Only twenty kilometres from Santiago de Compostela, O'Pedrouzo is popping at the seams. I take the side-streets to the albergue, which is all primary colours and angles, every one of its beds occupied.

Two women are folding laundry on their bunks. They seem to be mid-sixtyish but they could be younger. We are not an attractive bunch on the Camino. No makeup. Too much sun. Constant dehydration. They pay no attention to me as I arrange my belongings in the bright red cubby next to my bunk.

"It's the going unnoticed," says the one with the glasses. Her hair is silver, as if she's been turned upside down and dipped in mercury. She has the fine features of someone who must have turned many heads when she was younger. If I was a seventy-year-old man I'd ask her out in a heartbeat.

"You're right," says her friend. Or maybe they're not friends. Maybe they just met. They both have posh British accents. Like Victoria-the-medium.

"It's like wearing an invisibility cloak." She holds her glasses up to the light.

"Some days it's quite liberating though," says the brunette, rolling grey socks into a tiny ball. "Going to the shops without first showering or putting on mascara is something, isn't it?"

"When did it happen, do you think?" The silver-haired woman rubs her lenses with her T-shirt. "When did we go from being noticed to being part of the furniture?" She puts her glasses back on again, folds the last T-shirt. "At first I felt a kind of panic. I even tried Botox. But one day I glanced in the mirror and my right eyebrow was crooked. It was poking right up in the air, like a little hairy arrow directing traffic. That was the last day I injected that crap into my face." They both laugh as they leave the room, laundry done.

And I have a pilgrimage aha. I grew up invisible. Oh, I got plenty of recognition. I was after all a rule-following people pleaser. I was acknowledged. But not for my appearance. That was my sister's department. She caused the earth to quake simply by showing up and smiling. And that was fine. It allowed me to be the hard worker. Serious. Virtuous. Good. But Luna Blue made me visible in a different way. When that young woman at the club told me that I looked like Barbie, I felt, for the first time in my forty-eight years, beautiful. And in that moment, I understood what I never had before – that feeling *beautiful* is more powerful, by far, than feeling *good*.

But my shelf-life, as my husband pointed out after seeing Luna Blue on Jemma's iPhone, is limited. I am approaching invisibility. When Adam looked into my eyes and called me beautiful it was a dangerous thing. Because the power that comes with being thought beautiful is addictive. Specially if you're not used to it. It makes you believe, for a moment, that you are *not* aging, *not* mortal, *not* ordinary. Instead, it tricks you into imagining that you are special. Uncommon.

Oh my God. Is all this insanity simply my fear of getting old? Am I that superficial? Or is perimenopause messing with my head? The mammogram lady did say something about my hormones being confused. But surely I'm more than just a mixture of chemicals? Wouldn't someone with a destiny be above that sort of behaviour? Unless that *is* my destiny – madness. It does, after all, run in the family.

Fifteen was certainly a big year for me: confession, class captain, Sister Bernadette and Jonestown. It was also the year I found the scratches in the stink-wood table in Ouma's entrance hall.

I had walked by this table every summer vacation for years, never noticing anything out of the ordinary. But on this particular day the sun hit it at a different angle. And I saw, for the first time, the deep furrows in the wood, as if gouged in desperation. Or fury. Or by a wild creature, trapped.

"Wat het hier gebeur Ouma?" I asked. *What happened here?* Squatting in the sunlight, I ran my fingers across the grooves. They were wildly chaotic, yet meticulously precise.

"Dis jou mal ouma-grootjie" she said, checking the marble top for dust. *My mad great-grandmother?*

"Why was she mad?" I thought maybe Ouma was exaggerating. That it was a term of endearment. We were a funny family that way.

"Wie weet?" she said. *Who knows?*

Mental illness, like sex, was something you didn't talk about. If it appeared in your family, you kept it firmly locked in the barn, along with any illegitimate children and alcoholic uncles. Being on a farm probably made it easier to keep that kind of secret — unless, of course, you were the one living it. What made my great-grandmother carve those ribbons of anguish? Did anyone hold her tightly? Help her calm the Crazy?

One day, Ouma said, my great-grandmother walked down to the railway line and stepped in front of an approaching train, leaving behind a bereft husband, four-year-old daughter and two-year-old son — the grandpa I never met. What went through her mind as she stared death squarely in the eye? Or was the darkness so deep that she couldn't see anything beyond the approaching vortex of silence?

The sun has set on O'Pedrouzo. The hostel is still buzzing with pilgrims but I'm finding it easy to smile, say "Hola," and move on, without feeling obliged to have a conversation.

I finish my preparations for tomorrow. Everything I'll need in the morning is laid out, with the box of Band-Aids on top. I have kept Princess Jasmine for my walk into the cathedral. Jasmine is, by far, my favourite princess. I love her courage, her sense of adventure, her disdain for convention, her desire for freedom. And I adore her flowy chiffon pants.

I settle into my sleeping bag on the top bunk, thinking of the great-grandmother I never knew. The one who walked away, like a pilgrim, leaving her children playing in the farmhouse, her husband checking the vats of fermenting grapes. I imagine her on the tracks, in a black cloak, a bow at her neck. I see her face lit by the approaching train, her smile as she tugs at the bow. I feel the air move. And then she is gone.

Ouma never told me whether my great-grandmother died instantly. I envision her soul leaving her body in a graceful swirl, like the smoke that dances into the ethers when you blow out a candle.

Closing my eyes now, I see what I have not seen before: my great-grandmother's cloak on the railway line. The outside is black but the inside is filled with whorls of red and green and purple and yellow, like Joseph's coat of many colours. Like my tie-dye T-shirts.

As I fade into sleep I wonder: did she leave her multi-coloured cloak of madness draped across the tracks for someone else to pick up and slip on? Was that someone me?

There is no splash as I drop the baby in the swimming pool. She sinks, face down. Just before she reaches the bottom, her little body pivots and her eyes peer straight into mine. I am jolted awake. My eyes shoot open. I can never decipher my baby dreams. They come in many versions, but the theme is always the same: I kill the baby. And always I wake feeling ashamed. What kind of human being murders babies? Even in her dreams?

It's 4:30 am. Everyone is still asleep, leaving me alone with my murderous mind. I remember Sister Bernadette telling us, in catechism class, that if we were virtuous, and trusted in God we would always make the good choice. The right choice. But the right choice for whom? And is the right choice always the good choice? And what *is* virtue?

Two-and-a-half years after she humiliated me in front of my classmates, Sister Bernadette gave me a letter. It was the spring before high school graduation. The bell had just rung for the end of Latin. I did not enjoy Latin, but I loved the tiny classroom under the eaves. It had windows like the ones in Ouma's house. Depending on the season, the time of day and the humidity in the air, the wooden frames had to be shrugged open or closed, either with great force or extreme tenderness. I would stare at the sky outside the windows as we conjugated verbs in our sing-song teenage voices: "Amo, amas, amat, amamus, amatis, amant." *I love, you love, he loves, we love, you love, they love.* Despite all those years of conjugating, to this day both Latin and love remain a mystery.

That day, Sister Bernadette handed me a small white envelope as I was gathering my textbooks. She turned and left the room before I could say thank-you. I slipped it into my Latin-English dictionary and tried not to think about it until I got home later that afternoon.

Inside the envelope was one sheet of yellow stationery, the kind you buy in fancy boxes wrapped in cellophane. I flattened out the creases where it had been folded. In the top left corner was a yellow rose, the centerpiece of a little bouquet.

Lindy-Lou, it said, in Sister Bernadette's flowery nun handwriting. *I didn't get to know you until this year and I thank God for the knowledge. You were a wonderful pupil. Keep in touch please.*

The word *know* was heavily underlined. Why? Did Sister Bernadette know something about me that I didn't? What? And why would God have given *her* that knowledge? And why did it take him so long?

I didn't keep in touch. I wanted to forget Sister Bernadette. But she was impossible to exorcise, perhaps because I kept her letter. Folded exactly the same way as when she first gave it to me, thirty-four years ago, it's one of the three letters in Petunia's front pocket. I plan to burn it at the end of my pilgrimage, along with the rest of the shame I've accumulated.

As I wait for morning to come, I think of how Sister Bernadette got it all confused: distinguishing between right and wrong is not always simple. Sometimes people do horrible things in the name of God. Of freedom. Love. Good and bad aren't out there. They're inside us, all the time, shadow and light, twirling side-by-side in our hearts. Two wolves. And sometimes it's impossible to tell which is which. Despite our best intentions.

From my bunk I can just see the nightlight in the passageway. The bulb is covered with a frosted shade. The light flickers. I squint to get a better view and notice the ghostly vibrations: a moth, trapped. His wings flutter furiously. Then nothing. Like the moth that was extinguished backstage, the night I became Luna.

Sometimes it's the light that kills us.

21

It's still dark out, but I can't stay here any longer. Saint James is waiting. I gather my things quietly and make my way to the washroom. After brushing my teeth, I unwrap the Band-Aids. Princess Jasmine in her fantastic harem pants – turquoise, like my wedding dress. Like Tom's eyes. I wrap Jasmine around my toes and then it's socks and shoes. My ankle does not complain too much. This is good.

The empty Band-Aid box goes into the garbage can under the sink and I repack my toiletries. The just-in-case mascara! Saint James might appreciate the extra effort today. Leaning into the mirror, trying not to poke out my eye, I barely notice the door opening beside me. But I hear the exasperated sigh as a woman with mousy brown hair passes behind me. She shakes her head self-righteously at my early morning make-up session. Pilgrim judgement at its finest.

While the sanctimonious peregrina pees, I escape to the sofa in the dark foyer. Through the window I see two pilgrims walking by, their shells bobbing up and down on their backpacks. I dash after them as fast as my decrepit tendon will let me go – creepy stalker again. *And* wearing mascara, apparently a big pilgrim no-no.

The stars are still twinkling. What must it have been like that night, more than a thousand years ago, when Pelagius the hermit saw the ring of stars dancing in the night sky? Was he afraid? Did he know he was about to discover something wondrous? And just how *did* the Bishop verify that it was the remains of James the Greater lying in the forest? *Oh my God!* What if this pilgrimage is all one big hoax, created by a scheming clergy to entice travelers to Campus Stella, the Field of Stars? *Heresy!* I hear Sister Bernadette whisper.

In catechism class, I had learned about the three theological virtues: faith, hope and charity. Of the three, Sister Bernadette said, faith was the greatest, because there was nothing we ourselves could do to earn it. No deed holy enough. No sacrifice sufficient. Faith was a gift of grace from God himself, given to us freely, but only if we were open and willing to accept it.

I silence my blasphemous doubts about the authenticity of Saint James' bones, by gazing at the sky. Pilgrims talk about a special kind of energy on the Camino and this morning I feel it. Perhaps it's the dark, the flickering stars above. Hope. Backstage. Possibility.

While Christians claim the Camino as their own, pagans were walking this route long before Saint James or Jesus were born. Even the scallop shell predates Christianity. I had seen, in Sylvia's guidebook, Botticelli's famous painting, the Birth of Venus, in which the goddess Venus rises from the ocean on a scallop shell. The same scallop shell that enveloped Jesus' broken body in the church in O'Pedrouzo yesterday. What is it about human beings? This desire to *label* mystery as if doing so will grant us ownership? To possess the Way to righteousness – as if there were only one?

As the stars disappear, the road gets busier. I need not have worried about getting lost today. There are teenagers with boom boxes. Families with children running wildly back and forth. Young and old couples. Groups of men and women loudly shouting, "Buen Camino!"

"Buen Camino," I reply each time, forcing myself to smile and sound excited, not wanting to be *that* grumpy pilgrim. How different this must be from that first night – the hermit, the forest, the stars. Bones. Silence.

And suddenly, there it is. Saint James' final resting place. Santiago de Compostela. The Cathedral. I can't wait to see God! To get my instructions. It's 11 o'clock. The pilgrim service is at noon. I take my place in line with all the other pilgrims, hundreds of them it seems, all waiting to enter the church. So much talking, merry-making, jostling. What would Alfonso the Chaste think of this spectacle?

The apostle James' discovery had been the turning point for Christianity in Spain, which had until that time been confined to a very narrow portion of the Iberian Peninsula. The Muslim Moors occupied the rest. A kind of cult of Saint James began and the Camino de Santiago de Compostela became the most important Christian pilgrimage, after those of Jerusalem and Rome. It was during King Alfonso III's reign, between 866 and 910 AD that the chapel built by Alfonso II was replaced by a bigger church. Construction of the present cathedral, the one I'm about to enter, was started under the reign of Alfonso VI in the eleventh century.

Almost forty-five minutes after joining the lineup outside, I step through the cathedral's enormous wooden doors. It takes a while for my eyes to adjust to being inside again. *Holy crap! It's Vegas!* So many enormous statues, opulent rooms, the magnitude of it all, the shine. This would make the most fantastic backdrop for a burlesque show.

I sit on the cold marble floor, Petunia between my legs. *OK God*, I say. *I made it. Your turn.*

Nothing. From Heaven, I probably look like a pale beige dot. I try again, closing my eyes, hoping no one steps on me. I recite *Hail Mary* and *Our Father*, three times each in my head, the way I do every time I board a plane.

Still nothing. I've walked hundreds of kilometres with a fat ankle. I have endured snorers, shower fungi, and personal space invaders. I nearly died a hideous death on a snake-infested mountain and I have worn the same pair of shorts for far too many days in a row. I have knelt bare-legged in every ancient church in north-western Spain, spending precious euros on candles and God has not made the slightest attempt to acknowledge my efforts. I'm trying to be mature about it, but I'm feeling more than a little put out.

My Great Disappointment is interrupted by the men gathering in front of me. Eight of them. They lean in, whispering, conspiratorial, the folds of their red robes close enough for me to touch. What are they up to?

The robe closest to me is a deeper red than the others, almost purple. The man wearing it resembles my father, with his olive skin, black hair, silver wings on his temples and the deep lines on his forehead which somehow do not make him seem old, but ageless and wise instead. His eyes are closed. He opens them as an enormous silver chalice descends from above.

"The botafumerio!" The man beside me gasps.

Everyone oohs and aaahs. All eight men pull simultaneously on a collection of ropes sending the chalice back up to Heaven. It hovers briefly above my head, and then starts swinging back and forth across the length of the church, faster and faster until it seems to be racing at highway speed above me. If it falls now, I will be instantly killed. Its massive arc leaves behind trails of white smoke. *The Holy Ghost?* Rooted to the floor, I wait for my miracle. For God's voice. Any voice.

The botafumeiro stops swinging. The pilgrims around me are delighted. We are lucky to have seen it, they say. It isn't brought out for every pilgrim mass. And it is incense that it spits out, not the Holy Spirit. In days of old, before the invention of deodorant or albergues with showers, the incense served a purely practical purpose – to rid the church of pilgrim stench.

The red-robed men leave, my father's lookalike last in line. Priests and nuns file out behind them. The organ stops playing. All that is left is excited pilgrims. It feels like a bazaar. It would not surprise me to see pigtailed teenagers selling pop and donuts between the aisles. And still I wait.

With the cathedral emptying, I can now see Saint James. He is life size and as ostentatious as his surroundings, lit up via some kind of modern-day technological miracle. How many mines must have been emptied of gold and precious gems for the cathedral's construction? I stand, moving closer. Are those *arms* around his neck? *They're moving!*

"Creepy isn't it?" The voice next to me sounds like Earl Grey tea and cucumber sandwiches.

"It really is," I say, turning to her.

She has the kind of skin that was designed for the indoors. Pale and fine, gauze-like. But she has clearly failed to follow user instructions and has exposed it to all sorts of elements. The result is a web of fine lines covering every square inch of her face and neck, making her appear fragile, like Victoria-the-medium. The tendrils that have escaped from her ponytail are the colour of maple leaves in the fall. Her eyes are indigo in this light. They glow.

"Pilgrims hug Saint James in gratitude, for the journey completed," she explains. "The lineup is godawful, but it's not likely to get any better. Shall we go?"

I suspect no-one ever says *no* to those eyes, so I follow her. We move slowly up the stairs, behind the rest of the pilgrims, through elaborate golden archways. Dusting this place must be a nightmare. So many intricate curls and swirls and knobs and patterns – all gold. How many hungry mouths could the proceeds from just one of these baubles feed?

I scan the ornate statues, Saint James glittering on his throne, pilgrims worshiping at his feet, around his neck. Didn't God specifically forbid this? I remember Moses having a conniption when he descended Mount Sinai to find that his people had made a golden calf to worship in his absence. Maybe they were bored. Maybe afraid. Whatever the reason, Moses was furious. He broke those stone tablets, shattering the commandments to smithereens, that's how angry he was. How is this golden image of Saint James any different?

The statue is no less gaudy from the back than from the front. The woman with indigo eyes is ahead of me and I pay careful attention as she puts her arms around his neck. I must do this right. My destiny depends on it. She leans against the back of Saint James' head and all I can think of is the grubby pilgrim germs that will now be on her delicate cheek. She must be having the same thought, because she pulls away, making a gagging motion and laughter gurgles in my stomach. My moment with Saint James is ruined. Completely un-holy.

"Well, *that* was worth the wait," she says, as we leave the cathedral, rolling her eyes, which are even more remarkable in the sunlight. Dancing amethysts. "Do you have your Compostela?"

I haven't yet collected the piece of paper certifying that I have completed my pilgrimage.

"Good luck," she says, directing me to the Pilgrim's Office. "It'll be a long wait."

I watch her walk away. Underneath her fragile veneer, she is fierce – untamed. I imagine her rising naked out of the ocean on a scallop shell. *Venus.*

Despite her warning, the lineup for the Compostela is even longer than I expected. I have no choice but to wait. In the window opposite me is a poster: *Our Lady at the Cross* it says and it depicts Mary at the crucifixion. Jesus' body is nailed to the cross, blood dripping from his crown of thorns. Mary reaches towards him, anguish in her eyes. It's the universal story of suffering. Of great promise being battered into greater sorrow. Of a mother's inability to protect her child. Of life's transience, its unpredictability. A reminder that, in the blink of an eye, it could all be gone. Just. Like. That.

22

I was quietly minding my own business, reading a book on my little Eagle Harbour deck, when the call came. "This is the fire chief."

It seemed suddenly critical to pay attention to the clouds drifting by, the angle of the 5 o'clock sun, the shadows cast by the magnolia trees.

"There's been an accident. It's your son." He'd been hit by a car while riding his bicycle.

"Where?" I asked, as if making arrangements for a coffee date.

"On Marine Drive. At the school." A three-minute drive from our house.

My husband pulled into the driveway. From my seat on the deck, I could just about touch the side mirror on his truck.

"Thank-you," I ended the call with the fire chief.

"You need to go to the school," I said to my husband, through his open window. "I'll meet you at the hospital."

Without a word, he backed out of the driveway. It was going to be a beautiful sunset.

From my son's closet I pulled a pair of shorts, clean underwear, socks and a T-shirt. Then I collected his passport from the filing cabinet, his toothbrush from the bathroom and his runners lying at the front door. As if he were going on vacation. I couldn't find a bag the right size. They were all either too big or too small. I stood in the kitchen, waiting for God to hand me the perfect bag. When he didn't, I reached under the sink and pulled out a Safeway packet, hoping it wasn't the one that had had the T-bone steak in it earlier. Carting dead animal germs into a hospital was probably not a good idea.

I drove to the hospital, paid for parking and found emergency.

"Ma'am, you need shoes here," said the nurse, glancing at my naked feet.

I turned around, walked back to the parking lot, unlocked the trunk, and found my spare flip-flops. Then I called my husband. "Here."

"On my way," he replied. After so many years of marriage, words are used sparingly.

"How is he?" I asked.

"I don't know. They wouldn't let me see him." When he got to the scene of the accident, my husband was met by yellow tape. The road was closed, traffic re-routed. The emergency crew would not let him through. Once seen, the police officer had said, my husband would never be able to unsee his son's broken body. He was to go, instead, directly to the hospital and wait there for the ambulance.

There are probably couples who come together in times of crisis. My husband and I are not one of those. We pull apart. We waited for the ambulance, alone together, the Vancouver sun shining as if there would be no tomorrow.

The ambulance was missing in action. More than two hours had passed since the fire chief had called. Needing air, I went outside. The setting sun had turned the clouds red. Blood red. Was God up there, watching? Waiting for me to do something? Say something?

Just two days earlier I had been searching for safety pins. After looking in all the usual places, I remembered Luna Blue's stash in the toolbox. I pushed the seashells and old tax returns to one side and pulled the box from where it had been hiding in the dark.

As I opened it, Luna escaped. Costume jewellery twinkled between black stockings and satin gloves. Bobby pins, carpet tape and tiny scissors, needle and thread, the little tub of body glitter that I would never have reason to use again. And all those eyelashes. I missed the smell of the dressing room, waiting backstage, the camaraderie, belonging somewhere despite not belonging at all. Feeling sorry for myself, I'd sat weeping on the passage floor, a middle-aged drama queen bemoaning my life of ease.

Watching the darkening sky outside the hospital I wondered: was my son's accident my fault? Punishment for being selfish? Ungrateful? I went back inside, trying to leave behind my guilt.

"The cyclist's here," a nurse announced.

The paramedics wheeled him in on a stretcher. A sheet covered his injuries, but his feet were poking out. I did the same thing I did on the day he was born – counted his toes. Ten. They took him away. His father and I followed. Charts exchanged hands. Nurses attached needles and tubes and bags filled with liquid. Standing in the doorway, I made myself as small as possible while the flurry continued.

Then he was gone again, to a place where we were not allowed. There were procedures to be performed: X-rays, examinations, blood tests. A phone on the wall kept ringing. Who was calling? And why was no one answering? What if it was some terrible test result? Some irreparable damage that could not be undone?

When our son returned, he was sedated. Peaceful. I focused on the rise and fall of his chest. In. Out. All there is. And then the quiet came. No more doctors rushing around. The lights seemed a little dimmer. And the phone no longer rang.

I convinced my husband to go home. He needed to work in the morning. That's the thing about birth and death and accidents. While they can radically transform the trajectory of an individual's life, they have no impact whatsoever on the universe. Bills still have to be paid, flowers watered, pets fed.

"I'll let you know as soon as I hear anything," I said, as he leaned over our boy. He stared at him, long and hard. Then he left.

I remembered so clearly giving birth to this nine-pound, blue-eyed baby boy who never cried. An old soul, sent to teach me all sorts of things, he moved through life with a quiet strength, a courage that spoke of lifetimes of lessons, and a patience born of compassion. Never one to fuss, he went about the business of life stoically. He was a late talker, and even then, a reluctant one. I filled the silence by telling him stories.

At night, tucked behind him in his bed, I would make up tales about a king who shared his name. With my breath against his back, my arms around his toddler body, I would tell of the tribulations facing this imaginary sovereign, and how he always found the strength and resourcefulness to solve them. Scheming trolls and roguish knights were no match for King B's kindness and mystical intuition.

Why was magic my only solution to life's challenges? *Real* mothers knew that magic was impractical. As my boy drifted into sleep, his breath came from a deeper place.

Somewhere holy. Being witness to your child's breathing is a miracle you take for granted – until there is the possibility of losing it.

A nurse came into the room around midnight. She lifted the sheet to change the dressings and for the first time I saw my son's battered body. This child, who had been perfect at birth, had been sliced apart as if with a can opener. He didn't wake, or even move, as she cleaned his wounds. A train clickety-clacked across my ribs, squeezing the breath from my lungs.

The nurse tossed the soiled bandages in the bin at her feet. Every muscle in my body contracted. When she was finished, she pulled up the sheet and left, taking the bin containing pieces of my son with her. She said nothing. Not one word. I was invisible.

And then it was just me and my son again. We did not yet know the extent of his injuries. No one knew. But he was alive. It was that moment, waiting backstage in the dark, when anything could happen.

I wanted to climb up onto the bed and lie behind him, as I'd done when he was a toddler. To wrap my arms around him and whisper that everything was going to be fine. But there were too many bags with liquid, tubes running in and out of him. I couldn't even touch his fingers. Needles were taped to them, splints securing the bones presumed broken.

So instead, I made my body as big as I could, stretched my arms into wings, Mother as Avenging Angel, and leaned across his body, pouring my energy into this wise soul who never really belonged to me. And then I made a deal with God. Isn't that what mothers do?

I promised to be grateful, for my husband, my life in the suburbs. I would be happy. Relinquish my silly ideas of a Big Life. Stop climbing into strangers' vans and never again have lunch with a married man. Any man. If God would just make my son whole again.

"Señora! Señora!" I haven't been paying attention to the lineup's progress. It's my turn for the Compostela. I hand over my credencial to the young man behind the counter. He unfolds the concertina pages. There is a stamp from every albergue in which I've slept over the past three weeks. There are also stamps from some of the restaurants and churches I visited in the towns between. He counts the stamps to ensure I qualify for the Compostela.

During the ninth and tenth centuries, after Saint James' tomb was given official status as a pilgrimage destination, the scallop shell was used to certify that pilgrims had completed the Camino. But the shells were easy to falsify. Or purchase. So in the thirteenth century the Church replaced them with letters of proof, which later became the Compostela.

The young man reaches below the counter and retrieves a cream-coloured certificate. He stamps and dates it, proof that I have completed my pilgrimage. In fancy black letters, he writes my name: *Lindy-Lou.*

There should be thunder and lightning. Angels descending from Heaven. Something. *Any*thing to mark the occasion as special. Momentous. But nothing happens. Again.

Tomorrow I leave for Cape Finisterre, ninety kilometres away on Galicia's Atlantic coast. This was once believed to be the edge of the world, the place where the sun dies and the realms of the living and the dead merge. Since God has not yet instructed me on what to do with my little rocks, perhaps that is where I will leave them — the black one from the stream in Stanley Park, the white one from under the magnolia tree in my garden.

Many of the rocks along the Coast of Death are rumoured to have special powers. Some are able to determine whether people are guilty or innocent of serious crimes. Others warn of shipwrecks or other unhappy incidents in the future. But the rocks I am most interested in are the healing rocks the locals talk about, with the power to cure ailments of the head and the heart. Perhaps these rocks will have the answers I'm seeking, since God has been consistently silent.

My ankle is complaining, so I manoeuver my way through the crowds in search of a bed. Almost every second doorway leads to a pub or a restaurant, or some other place filled with people. Everyone seems happy. Beatific, somehow. Did God show up for all them? Just not for me? And is it because I broke the promise I made that night in the hospital?

For a while there, both God and I kept our side of the bargain. But one day it all came tumbling down.

All that trying to be happy and grateful had not worked. So, as the sun rose on my fifty-first birthday, I wrote my husband the letter, telling him that I did not love him the way a good wife should. That I needed to leave, to find the life that had been intended for me all along.

When I left that letter next to him on the bed, and walked out the door, I was effectively reneging on the deal I'd made with God. But I was lucky. My husband read the letter, found me outside, next to the dead daisies, and gave me a reprieve – the Camino. Being a pilgrim was my chance to make amends. It also allowed me to believe, for just a while longer, that I had not broken my promise. But God isn't stupid. He knows the truth.

CAMINO FINISTERRE

O body swayed to music, O brightening glance,
How can we know the dancer from the dance?
~W.B. Yeats

23

I'm awake at 6 o'clock and on the cobblestones in minutes. Yesterday it was impossible to escape the hordes. This morning I'm alone outside the cathedral. And now I can see its magnificence. It's comforting to think of the thousands of pilgrims who have walked through the cathedral doors before me. In search of answers. Absolution too, perhaps. While I like to believe that my turmoil is mine alone, I am of course not that extraordinary. On the surface our lives may appear as unique as our fingerprints, but at our cores we are all simply trying to do the same thing: find our way.

It seemed so easy, at fifteen: if I followed the rules, my destiny would be revealed and, with God's blessing, I would forge ahead and fulfil it. But a lot has happened since then. Mistakes made. Rules broken, sometimes not accidentally.

I adjust my shoes and start walking, keeping an eye out for scallop shells to point me in the right direction. With the sun not quite risen, my legs are chilly in my shorts.

A flash of black crosses my path, followed by another. Cats! They disappear down an alley. Is something chasing them? Glancing around, I spot the painted yellow arrow. Almost hidden in the early morning light, it is directing me down the same alley. Is it a trick? There's no shell. Just an arrow. I hear my husband's voice, warning me about criminals lying in wait for unsuspecting pilgrims. But I follow the arrow anyway.

It seems suddenly darker. Colder. I walk faster. The houses are so close by, surely no one would think of murdering me here? Anyone could be peeking out of their windows. Where *are* the windows? Are those footsteps behind me?

The footsteps grow louder. If I'm going to be hacked to pieces I might as well stare my fate in the eye. As I turn around, something furry runs between my legs and I topple over.

"You OK, mate?" I recognise that voice. "Here, let me give you a hand," he says, as cats of all sizes and colours rub against me where I'm sprawled in the alley.

I have no option but to let Tasmanian Tom pull me up. My butt is freezing, and the cats are not letting up.

"You found the shortcut. Well done, Canada!" he says, as though I'm two years old.

I dust myself off.

"Hang on a sec." He swipes at the dirt on my calves. "Okay, you're good now. Let's get out of this alley."

He is so infuriating. I'm not a toddler. I can clean my own self. But it's too early in the morning, and too cold to take a stand, so I follow Tom obediently out of the alley.

As we leave the cats and Santiago de Compostela behind, the path takes us into a forest. And Tom does that thing again, the thing he did the day we met in Boente: he walks in sync with me, matching me stride-for-stride, despite my uneven gait. It is both upsetting and comforting.

"Look!" He stops without warning, picks a leaf from the ground and pokes it under my nose.

"What?" *It's a leaf for goodness' sake.*

"Look at the trees," he says.

It's the Concours de Ballet all over again – my ballet teacher telling me to look at the tappers' ankles. And me clueless about what I'm looking for.

"Do you see any leaves shaped like this?" Tom asks.

I don't. All the trees around us have broad, wavy leaves, like the amoeba I used to doodle in Biology class. The leaf Tom is holding is pointy, sort of arrow-like.

"Where do you think this came from?" he asks, excited.

It tricks me, this expression of wonder on his face and I hear myself say, "Let's see if we can find out." Too late, I remember my mother's caution about curiosity killing the cat and, cursing myself, I head into the woods with Tom. Flora is not really my thing. My ankle is sore and I will need to pee soon. A sudden swirl of wind makes me shiver.

"Look!" Tom shouts. Head up-tilted, arms outstretched, he is spinning in circles, exactly as I did on my first day in Portugalete, when I couldn't decide whether to take the walkway. As he twirls, pointy leaves rain down on him. I am briefly transfixed. "I found it," he beams.

"No, you didn't," I say. "*It* found *you*." I cannot let Tom sidetrack me. I'm here to find my future, not a bothersome man. I stomp out of the forest. Tom follows me. Why is he causing me such agitation? Is it because he reminds me of Adam?

A few days after my son was discharged from hospital, on his way to recovery, I visited my favourite cemetery in North Vancouver. The one thing that could silence the Crazy was dead people.

As I exited the highway, there was a honk behind me. It was Adam, waving at me from his tomato-red car. My solar plexus fluttered, like the butterflies that used to dance in my ballerina tummy as I waited backstage. I wanted to ignore him, but I couldn't. That would be plain rude. So I returned his wave before entering the cemetery.

I parked under a tree sprouting new leaves and found the bench erected in loving memory of someone's father and grandfather. A man called Roy. Roy's bench had spectacular views of the North Shore mountains.

While the past months had been spent focusing on my family and on being grateful, I still thought about Adam. I had never stopped wondering why he'd walked into *my* driveway that long-ago day. What was it that made him whisper into *my* sweaty ear? Could he see the cracks? The confusion? Was it something I did? Or was it purely circumstantial? If it wasn't me he happened to cross paths with that afternoon, could it just as easily have been some other woman in some other driveway? I suspected so.

I was just settling in on Roy's bench, when there was a hand on my neck. "You OK?"

I jumped, my skin on fire under Adam's fingers.

He walked around the bench, sat next to me. "Good to see I have that effect on you."

The flush spread to my cheeks.

"You know someone here?" he asked.

"No," I said, acutely aware of how weird that must seem.

"So you come here for fun?"

I laughed. He did too. The heat in my face evaporated. We watched, side-by-side, the clouds chasing each other across the mountains.

When I spoke, what popped out of my mouth surprised me. "Do you love your wife?"

"Yes," he said, not hesitating. "I do."

"Then why did you say that stuff to me in the driveway?" I wanted him to know how his words had tormented the Crazy in my spine.

"Because it's true," he said. "I have always been attracted to you."

"But you're happily married?" What was I missing?

"Yes. Aren't you?"

And so I told him. In the graveyard, on Grandpa Roy's bench. That I was a bad wife. Because I was never meant to be one. Adam put his arm around my shoulder, pulled me closer. He felt solid in the silence. Leaning into him, I wondered why, if God could fix my son, he could not simply take away my Crazy. Just poke his almighty finger into my marrow and pull it out. Leaving me normal. Sane. Happy.

My bones grew heavier, my tiredness sinking into Adam's body as the clouds cast shadows at our feet. A helicopter whirred somewhere above. Still we did not move.

"Do you know how beautiful you are?" Adam said, long after the helicopter had spun away.

I pulled away, perplexed.

"Inside and out," he said, taking my hands in his, the way Victoria-the-medium had done. He looked at me. No, *into* me. As if I was the only person in the world who mattered. Even though he'd just told me he loved his wife. It was as though he could see the war going on in my heart. And it didn't frighten him.

When I got home, hours after the unplanned graveyard rendezvous, there was a note from Adam in my mailbox. My driveway letter.

Tom and I have seen no other pilgrims since leaving Santiago de Compostela. I am still torn between wanting to be rid of him and hoping he'll stay. Being lost is a lot less scary when you have company.

The trees make way for little rectangular buildings beside the road, some on stilts, some on stone blocks, all raised high above the ground. Like enlarged coffins.

"They're hórreos," Tom says, even though I haven't asked. "Like an Oreo, but emphasizing the e. You know Oreos?"

Of course I know Oreos. These are not cookies. "But what are they?"

"They're mini granaries." How does he know this? "By building them high above the ground you keep the rats away."

"Oh, so they're not for dead people," I say out loud, by mistake.

He doesn't laugh. Instead, he says, "Do you spend a lot of time around dead people?"

"Not really." It's none of his business that I hang around cemeteries.

"I do," he says, and I can feel him waiting for me to ask.

I don't. I do not want to know this story. Even if it includes death. *Specially* if it includes death. I do not want Tom leaking vulnerability all over me. Because that will just mess with my head.

Out of nowhere, a stone bridge appears. On the other side of it, is an ancient village. Stone streets, stone houses,

stone walls. The only sound is the waterfall. It cascades into
the river, then passes under the bridge through five arches.
Tom and I cross into the village quietly, as if one too-loud
step will make it disappear. Like Brigadoon. There are
flowers and hedges. And curtains in the windows. But not
one living thing walking about. No cats, no cows, no
humans. A fountain is carved into a stone wall at the end
of the road. We fill our bottles and sit side-by-side on the
bench, muted by the otherworldliness of it all.

"This is what it feels like on the ward sometimes," Tom
says. "As though all those sick babies – all that sadness and
suffering – can't possibly be real."

I adjust my shoelace, trying to stop Tom's story. But he
goes on, encouraged, I suspect, by the eeriness that hangs
heavy, like the vines above our head. "You keep hoping
that if a rooster just crows, or someone snaps their fingers,
everything will go back to the way it was. The way it's
meant to be."

I focus on the bridge while Tom talks about his work in
the neonatal intensive care unit. He's a pediatric surgeon.
His days are filled with premature babies. Sick babies.
Dying babies.

"You know they're not going make it. But sometimes it
takes weeks or even months before they die. And all the
time their parents are hoping. Praying. Believing it'll be
okay. That all their suffering will be worth it."

Shivers run across my forearms. My neck. My temples.

"But all there is, is more pain." His voice is
unemotional, matter-of-fact, as though he's talking about
knitting.

I stand, trying to push away the image of dead babies.
There are enough of those in my dreams. Tom follows.

It is a peculiar day, a prelude of sorts somehow. Like
going to the ballet with my father, when I would rush to
the orchestra pit as the musicians took their places for the

pre-performance warmup. I was captivated by the way they held their instruments, turned the sheet music, tuned strings, polished cymbals. There was no melody. Just individual notes, beats, rhythms. But it was thrilling. When the warmup finished, I would take my seat beside my father again, knowing that despite what I had just experienced, I still had no inkling of what was about to happen.

That's how today feels. How Tom feels.

24

The clear blue sky this morning gives no hint of the downpour that forced us into a horrible little hostel on the outskirts of Negreira yesterday. The whole place smelled of fried chicken and wet dog. I went to sleep early last night, to avoid the busyness of the place, and knowing too much about Tom. The rain pounded against the roof all night.

Tom and I left early this morning, bound to walk together by the story he told me yesterday. Because that's what stories do. They connect you in a way nothing else can – with invisible chains of shared humanness. Which is why they are so perilous.

We have again met no other pilgrims along the route today. It is a most peculiar thing, this absence of pilgrims while you walk and then the glut of them when you arrive at your next destination.

On the side of the road, we come upon a wooden cross, about three feet high, with three little rocks in front of it. No name, no dates, only the words *mi alma gemela para siempre* etched in the wood.

"You read Spanish?" Tom asks.

I shake my head, no.

"My soulmate forever," Tom translates triumphantly.

I am usually polite to a fault, but "hmmph" pops out.

"What? You don't believe me?"

"Oh, I believe you," I shake my head. "It's the soulmate thing that's stupid."

He raises one eyebrow. "Interesting. I pegged you as a soulmate kinda girl."

"And what, exactly, is that?" I don't disguise my irritation. How can he peg me as *any*thing? He's the one who's been blurting his sad stories all over the place, not me. He doesn't know a thing about me.

"Someone who believes in magic," he says, ignoring my exasperation. "And fairy tales. Happily-ever-after. Eternal love. That sort of thing."

I press my lips together tightly, to prevent another *hmmph* from escaping.

"So you don't believe in soulmates?" he says when I don't answer.

"I have some issues with love."

"Like what?"

"It's complicated," I say, thinking of Ouma.

I was fourteen – the exact age my mother had been when her father died. Ouma and I were in the garden, picking hydrangeas, when she casually mentioned that when my grandfather died, she had begged God to take all her children if she could just have her husband back. I thought

I'd misunderstood, and stared at my grandmother as if seeing her for the first time.

"Ek het gebid," she said. *I prayed.* She moved on to the next hydrangea bush, clippers ready. I followed, carrying the tin bucket. "Every morning and every night. On my knees. Next to my bed. Our bed. I didn't want my children. I wanted my husband."

Did my mother and her brothers know? Did they sense their mother's desperation to have not *them*, but their dead father, by her side? I couldn't fathom a love so deep that you would trade your children for it. If that's what having a soulmate meant, I wanted no part of it. A sword and a purpose sounded so much simpler. Safer. Less painful.

"Yeah, love is fucked up," Tom says, as the bay of Cee appears before us, dotted with boats. "I never would have guessed that my wife had it in her to cheat."

Goddammit! How am I meant to focus on my own drama when Tom has so many upsetting stories?

"I'd just lost a baby," Tom says as we get to the beach. "His name was Garrett." He drops his pack on the sand and sits beside it.

I do the same with Petunia.

"He'd been fighting for three weeks." Tom stretches his legs out in front of him. "He had such a huge heart."

A seagull squawks above us.

"But that morning, he gave up the fight."

We watch the gull.

"It was a Wednesday."

The bird joins us on the beach.

"Garrett's parents were shattered."

The gull picks at scallops in the sand. Can't he see they're dried out? Lifeless?

"*I* was shattered," Tom says quietly.

During his silence I focus on the cove – an accidental bystander as he relives that day.

"I barely noticed the bicycle next to the garage when I got home."

One boat is racing to the ocean, its red and yellow sail flapping merrily in the breeze.

"I went upstairs to shower. When I opened the bathroom door, Gloria was leaning into the tiles under the shower head, her arms spread wide."

Suddenly, all the boats seem to be trying to escape to sea.

"At first I thought she was in pain. Crying. Then I saw the fucker."

Tom doesn't speak again. I can't leave him there in the bathroom, with Gloria and the fucker, and his dying marriage, so I say, "What did you do?"

He smiles. "I flushed the toilet."

The seagull flies off.

"Then I went downstairs, grabbed a beer and turned on the TV."

"And then?" I can't imagine the pandemonium upstairs.

"It was fucking figure skating."

We both laugh. Then silence again. All the boats have made it to sea.

"Did you know him?" I ask. Does betrayal cut deeper when it's someone we know, rather than a stranger?

"Yeah. He's an artist. Bob. Bob Burnett." He says the name slowly, exaggerating the vowels, turning Bob into a cartoon character. "Gloria had dragged me to some of his shows." Tom flexes his feet, one at a time. "Then she signed up for painting classes with him." He rotates his ankles. Clockwise. Then anti-clockwise. Like we used to do in ballet class. "They'd been fucking for more than a year when I caught them."

I want to pat Tom's arm. Lean my head on his shoulder. Hug him. I don't.

"You know what the worst thing is?" Tom says, shaking his legs. "He rides a bicycle! *That* just screwed with my head. That my wife would fall in love with someone who doesn't even own a fucking car."

"So *is* it love?" I ask, wondering how certain you can ever be. Love takes time. It's not champagne and chocolate and walks in the park. Or sex in the shower. It has to survive in the cold light of paying bills, getting sick, doing laundry.

"Who knows?" he shrugs. "She says she loves him, but she's a narcissist. And narcissists aren't capable of loving other people."

Oh my God! That's what I am! A narcissist! I suddenly see how self-involved I've been. I have left behind my family in Vancouver to traipse through Spain on my own to find my destiny. That's the kind of thing adolescents do. Not old ladies!

"Christ!" Tom says.

"What?" I'm thankful to have something other than my narcissism to think about.

"Your ankle is purple!"

"Oh, it's been like this for ages." I unlace my shoes. "It'll be fine once I soak it in the ocean."

Tom removes his shoes too and we head towards the water, the only people on the beach.

"Do you hate your wife?" I ask him as we reach the sea.

He shakes his head. "I was furious with her when I found out what she'd been doing. But then it was like this unshackling. She needed more than I could give her." He takes two more steps into the sea. "More than I *wanted* to give her. And now I feel less burdened. I'm not constantly reminded of what a bad husband I was."

"Was it always like that? Feeling not enough?" I ask him, knowing exactly how this feels.

"I'm not sure," he says as we stand side-by-side in the water. "I don't think it was always like that. But one day I realised I cared more about my work than I did about my wife. I cared more about a lot of other things. It was probably a million little decisions – mostly mine – that got us there."

Tom is right. The course of a marriage is charted by barely perceptible steps. It's the big things that shine a light on it. But it's the tiny things, piled one on top of the other, that make it what it is. Or isn't.

"Let's have a look at your ankle," he says, and I follow him back to our pile of belongings on the beach. We sit opposite each other in the sand, my foot in Tom's hands.

"This hurt?" He prods the squishy bits.

I shake my head, no.

His fingers wrap around my ankle and as he touches my Achilles, pain shoots up my leg. My flinch tells him what he needs to know. "Yeah, you shouldn't be walking."

"Tell that to God," I say, pulling my foot towards myself.

"I don't believe in God," Tom says as we pull on our shoes and socks.

"But you're a doctor." I'm not sure how the two are connected. It just seems that all the miracles you'd see as a doctor would make you a believer. Like two flawed mortals creating life. That's surely reason to believe in something bigger than yourself? Even a narcissist like me can see that.

"I've seen too many babies suffer." He unzips his backpack and pulls out two ice packs. "If there *was* a God, he'd be able to prevent that."

Tom's rationale is one I've heard before. But I can't imagine not believing in God. I have lived my entire life trying to please him, in perpetual fear of his wrath. Expecting to be punished for my sins, rewarded for my piety.

Tom hands me the ice packs and points to the diagrams explaining how to crack them to release the cold. "Use one tonight and one tomorrow."

I unzip Petunia to pack them away and my rocks fall out.

"You've got *rocks* in your backpack?" Tom says.

I glare at him, with what I hope is a bold stare, though it's probably not.

"Where are they from?" he asks.

"Vancouver."

"You brought rocks from *Canada*? Why?"

I can't tell Tom that the white rock is my husband, and everything else I should be grateful for. Or that the black rock is Adam, and all my other transgressions. He'll laugh at me. So I say: "It's what pilgrims do."

He laughs anyway. "Would you like me to carve you a cross to carry on your back too, while you're at it?"

I roll my eyes at him, zip up my rocks and walk back to the road. Tom follows, still laughing.

At the top of the hill we find ourselves in a courtyard, surrounded by ancient walls. Not a sound drifts in from the surrounding streets. It's as if we are alone in the world. A grey stone church blocks our way. An enormous clock above its wooden doors is flanked by two white crosses. Seven little turrets are each topped by a stone cross. A final, tenth cross, rests above the entrance.

"Fuck. That's a lot of crosses," Tom says.

"Coming in with me?"

"Hell no. I haven't been in a church in forty years. It would take one of your God's miracles to get me in there."

He hugs me goodbye. "Take care of yourself, kiddo. I'll look for you in Finisterre."

Tom is continuing on to Finisterre today, but I'm staying in Cee. It's a full moon. And I have a ritual planned.

I watch him walk into the alley. Just before he disappears, he turns around. The sun is behind him, so I can't see his face, only his silhouette. He raises his hand, and shouts, "Get rid of the fucking rocks, Canada! They're not making things easier on that ankle!" And then he's gone.

Inside, the church is stark, completely unlike Santiago's cathedral. A plain white cloth covers the stone altar. Behind the altar, instead of Jesus, is a window shaped like a flower, each petal a slightly different colour glass. A kind of muted tie-dye effect. My kind of church.

From the front pew I glance into the alcove on the right. It's the man in the black hat! The one who glared disapprovingly at me from behind the altar in Boente, just before I met Tasmanian Tom. The large book he carried under his arm there, is now open on his lap. He sits on a throne of gold, pen suspended in mid-air, as if about to pronounce judgement.

And suddenly I recall Victoria-the-medium's words. *The only one judging you, is yourself,* she'd said as I cried. I study the man in the black hat, with disappointment and judgement in his eyes. I had thought he was my husband. But I see now – the man in the black hat is me.

25

The citizens of Cee are clearly immune to pilgrim shenanigans. No one even glances at me as I create a large shell circle on the beach, not far from where Tom told me, earlier today, about his wife's betrayal. Has Tom arrived in Finisterre? Will I ever see him again?

When the circle is complete – fifty-two whitewashed shells spaced as evenly as possible – I sit cross-legged in the centre. The sand surprises me with its coldness. It was so warm when Tom and I sat here, just a few hours ago.

I have been collecting scallops since Laredo, when Nico and Sylvia and I missed the pilgrim blessing because we stayed on the beach too long. I have gathered one for each year I've been alive and one for the future. These are the fifty-two shells that form the circle around me. It's hard to believe I'm so old and still so clueless. I know less now, than I did when I left high school. I still remember all those youthful dreams. But my father's sword is gone and I have not lived up to the expectations of my name. Not even remotely.

The moon is hiding behind the mountains so I can't see the boats in the bay. But I can hear them bobbing on the water. Like Vancouver, there are no waves here. After nearly two decades of no longer calling South Africa home, I still miss the wildness of the Indian ocean. I remember my children's disappointment, too, the first time we visited the beach in West Vancouver.

"Where's the sea?" my five-year-old son asked.

"Right there," I pointed to the calm surface.

"That's a lake," said my daughter who, at age three, knew everything.

"No, that's the sea," I said.

"But where are the waves?" asked my son again.

"There aren't any waves in Vancouver," I explained.

"Then it's not the sea," said the girl-child confidently. "And anyway, this isn't a beach."

Sweet Jesus. "Yes, it is. It's Ambleside Beach."

"No, it's not. There's no sand, only stones. Beaches have white sand," she pouted.

Her brother was silent, his thoughts safely tucked inside his head where no one could touch them.

My daughter was right, though. In terms of beaches, Ambleside was disappointing. But of course, I couldn't agree with her. My job, as the mother, was to pretend that everything was perfect. Tearing our children away from their family and friends, their belongings and their seaside home in a sunny climate, had to be worth the effort. If *I* couldn't be excited about Vancouver, how could I expect *them* to be happy? So, in a state of pathological enthusiasm, that first day on the beach with my African children, we chased crabs, hunted gigantic purple starfish and collected shells. They had to love this place.

"Do you know why there aren't any waves here?" I asked later, when we were packing our shells into the empty cracker box for safekeeping.

"Why?" said my daughter, still quite disgruntled by it all.

"Because mermaids live here."

"Really?" Her eyebrows made big question marks.

"Yes," I moved closer to her. "There are whole families of mermaids out there. And they'd get tossed about if there were waves. Maybe get hurt."

She climbed into my lap, staring at the water.

"Do you see that little man?" I pointed to the inukshuk on one side of the beach, a stone figure built by balancing rocks, one on top of the other. Traditionally used by the indigenous people in Arctic North America, as landmarks and means of communication, inukshuks can be found on most of Vancouver's shoreline, created by anyone with sufficient time and patience.

"Yes?" She looked at the man of stone.

"He's keeping watch. When everyone's gone home, and there are no more people on the beach, he lets the mermaids know. And when the moon comes out tonight, they have a mermaid party on the rocks."

Squinting at the horizon, she twirled her hair with her finger. Her toddler body melted into mine as she whispered, "Maybe we could hide one night and watch their party."

I smiled into her neck. "Maybe we could, sweetpea. Maybe we could."

My son was silent. He lifted my hand from where it was resting on the beach, uncurled my fingers and put a shell in my palm. Then he closed my fingers around the shell and sighed. It sounded like peace.

As long as we could collect shells we'd be alright.
Wouldn't we?

I am surrounded by shells. One enormous scalloped circle
on the beach in Cee, containing the Crazy.

It's the first anniversary of my son's accident. Exactly
three hundred and sixty-five days ago I stood over his body
in the hospital and made a deal with God. Because I
believed God could hear my prayers. Could answer them.
But here on the cold Spanish sand, with the moon playing
hide and seek, and God being equally elusive, I am struck
by a thought: what if everything I've ever believed is a giant
myth? What if Tom is right? What if there is no God?
What *then?*

Sacrilege, the little voice in my head hisses. So I push
away the thought and find the white candle and the yellow
lighter I bought at the Dollar Store this afternoon.

Before leaving Vancouver, I'd Googled 'full moon
gratitude rituals.' I found Violet, the New England Witch.
Her blog was wondrous. There were rituals for navigating
sudden change or attracting the perfect job. I skipped over
finding your soulmate – that seemed like a waste of time.

The spell for working mermaids briefly distracted me.
It guaranteed a tail and mermaid powers and I even had all
the necessary ingredients in my kitchen cupboards. But
Violet didn't clarify whether the transformation was
temporary or whether the mermaid tail would be forever.
I could imagine the chaos that would cause in Safeway. So
I moved on.

The full moon gratitude ritual seems simple enough.
With a pointy rock from the beach, I engrave *thank-you* on
the candle, trying not to think about all the awkward

situations associated with this word. Violet's website suggested writing a gratitude list, but there was no space in Petunia for pens and paper. Anyway, the spell is only complete once the candle burns all the way down, so this will give me time to recite my gratitude list. And saying it out loud seems somehow more ceremonial than simply writing it. More pilgrimly.

The sky is thick with cloud. Where is the moon? Knowing it's there is poor substitute for actually seeing it. Not unlike God. I flick the lighter. The flame illuminates the *thank-you* etched in the wax, and I think of all the things I have been gifted. Home. Health. Children. Husband. I list all my extended family members. I say thank-you, deeply, for my son's returned wholeness. For my pilgrimage. The conversations I've had. Friends. All the undeserved privilege that is my life. I understand how grateful I should be.

My hands are numb. My nose is running. Why did I buy such a fat candle? Shoving my fingers into my armpits for warmth, I close my eyes and yawn. A giant soul-stretching yawn. When I open my eyes, the clouds are gone. The moon is so low, it feels as though I could climb right into it. And all around, the sky is navy, turning the moon blue. Luna Blue.

I still miss her. Fearless, unapologetic Luna.

My husband thought my foray into burlesque meant that I was broken. He didn't understand that I was broken long before that. What burlesque did, was introduce me to a self so unexpected that it took my breath away. Being honest with ourselves is the hardest kind of truth there is. Coming face to face with your brutally naked soul is oftentimes not terribly pretty. And Luna forced me to do that. By inviting the black wolf to dance.

The candle hisses and dies. *Finally!*

With the moon now full and luminous over the little cove in Cee, I gather my shells. When I get back to Vancouver I will add them to the collection in the passage cupboard, beside the toolbox containing Luna Blue's remains – my reminder that I once had courage.

26

I'm not sure if it's Tom's icepack or last night's ritual in the cold, but as I slide my foot into my shoe, gritting my teeth in anticipation, there is … nothing! My ankle is still fat, but for the first time since Güemes, seventeen days ago, it doesn't hurt when I stand on it. A full moon miracle!

It's only fourteen kilometres to Finisterre. The road is flat and slightly higher than sea level, so the trees don't obscure my view of the ocean. It's hard to believe that I am almost at the end of my pilgrimage. In two days, I will begin the return trip to Canada – still no wiser.

I force my legs to slow down. They seem anxious to get to the Ends of the Earth, but I'm in no rush. I want to meet someone today. I'm not sure who. I'm hoping for a story that I can hold onto as my last pilgrim encounter. But the road stays quiet.

There is an African proverb that says *when you pray, move your feet*. And that is what I have done on the Camino. Every morning, I have woken up and put one foot in front of the other. Over and over. And waited for God to answer me.

I am still waiting, still moving my feet, still hopeful, but time is running out.

In the distance, I see someone walking towards me. My person! The sun is angled into my eyes, so it's mostly silhouette approaching. Is that a scythe? Am I hallucinating? Only Death carries a scythe.

As I get closer, I see it's a woman, an old woman, at least eighty, with deep wrinkles on her cheeks and forehead. Balanced on her head is what resembles Jack's entire magic beanstalk. It must weigh at least fifty pounds! The scythe dangles loosely from her one hand. It's probably what she used to hack the vegetation she's transporting on her head.

Despite the scythe, she is unlike any Grim Reaper I've ever seen. Fuzzy brown socks reach halfway up her shins, and her plastic clogs are covered in mud. Her floral dress is protected by a blue-and-white checked apron with bulging pockets. On her little grey head, underneath the mass of greenery, is a faded green crocheted hat, angled just so. The morning light catches her dewdrop earrings, turning them into mini chandeliers making fairy dances on the asphalt. The hand holding the scythe starts swaying back and forth, as if it is preparing to hack something else. She comes closer.

Her eyes are black. It's the kind of black that you wish you could climb into, because you sense that in that blackness lies a truth you have never before known. Even if she wanted to kill me, I would not run.

She lifts her hand, the one without the scythe, and rests it on my cheek, in exactly the same way I imagine my great-grandmother would have done with her children before she walked towards the train. A kind of stillness fills me. Unlike the Crazy, which dances first in my coccyx before tripping up my backbone, this feeling of warmth starts at the top, as if there is a hole in the centre of my skull, and golden lava is being poured into it.

In these black eyes, I see the woman outside Starbucks, wearing red Converse like mine, digging for the truth in her shopping cart. This woman, with the beanstalk on her head, her hand on my cheek, has found it. I want, so badly, for her to tell me what it is. But all she says, as her fingers touch my face, is "guapa." She does not smile.

After what seems like forever, and yet not long enough, she removes her hand from my cheek and continues on her way. I watch her, the spaces between my vertebrae somehow softened. And then I turn, once again, towards Finisterre, where it sits at the end of a bay shaped exactly like the old woman's scythe.

Between my eyes and the ocean is a kind of magnetic energy. In a mesmerised march, I arrive in the seaside town before the albergues are open. Which is how I end up in a room-with-a-view and a private bathroom, feeling positively queenly.

The young woman who shows me to my room is apologetic. "The lighthouse is covered in fog right now," she says, as if it's her fault.

The weather today does not concern me, I tell her. I'll be spending another two days in Finisterre, performing all my pilgrim rituals. The first one involves clams.

She directs me to the Pirate Restaurant: "The best clams in town." As she leaves, I remember to ask her what guapa means.

"Beautiful."

Beautiful? This was not the word I was expecting. Guapa was meant to mean something fantastic and mystical. Profound. Something to match the truth I spied in the old woman's eyes. Not beautiful.

Disappointed, I enter the bustling centre of Finisterre. It is filled with tourists and reminds me of Santillana del

Mar, where I vomited at the wedding. But it's less shiny, more ramshackle. I turn left towards the ocean, as directed, and almost collide with a dilapidated staircase. At the top of the stairs a barrel with skull-and-crossbones and *Pirata* painted in large white letters indicate that I'm at the right place. A toothless chef with hoop earrings and an eye patch balances a bright green parakeet on his shoulder. The walls inside are the exact shade of my orange hiking shoes.

I order a bottle of water and a dozen clams, which arrive at my table too quickly, causing me to break into a sweat. Things in shells make me anxious. Why am I doing the clam ritual? All I can recall is that I have to toss a dozen clamshells into the ocean. Will it still count if I empty the shells without actually eating the little critters? Or is that cheating?

Scraping out their insides, I make a little clamshell mountain on the paper napkin. Then I cover the clams with rice to disguise their fishiness, and chew and swallow the lot as quickly as I can. After gulping down the entire bottle of water, I leave the restaurant with my clamshells, congratulating myself on a task well done.

On the street corner, a man with a blackened apron is dunking pastry in a steel tub filled with sizzling oil. He drops five fat doughy fingers into a square sieve. When he lifts them out again they are bronze. Shiny.

"Churros?" he says.

"Churros?" I repeat. He must think I'm an idiot. What are churros? Besides oil on a stick?

He shoos flies off the newspaper beside him. With one hand, he tears a page, folds it in half, wraps it around a pastry finger and hands it to me.

I ignore the clams twitching in my stomach and take a bite. *Oh!* This is champagne in Stanley Park. The pastry is filled with melted chocolate. I gobble it quickly, eliminating the last clammy remnants from my taste buds, and buy four more.

By the time I get back to my room, all five pastries have joined the clams and rice in my stomach. All hell breaks loose shortly after, while I'm rinsing my socks in the pink basin in the bathroom.

It seems a peculiar kind of retribution to spend my first night at the Ends of the Earth hanging over a toilet bowl. At 5 am, just as night is turning to day, I sink into bed, fully purged after ten hours of vomiting.

The sun on my face wakes me at noon. Noon!

The T-shirt and shorts I washed before I started throwing up, are draped on wire hangers, the first hangers I've seen since leaving Vancouver. Socks are drying on the windowsill. A lone picture hangs crookedly on the wall, as if it was once part of a family of prints, now lost or broken. Surely not stolen? A woman with an Audrey Hepburn updo sits with her back to the artist on a powder blue couch. Draped in a white sheet, her back naked, she is fragile. I bet she couldn't walk the Camino.

I want to lie here for a while longer, but I have a lighthouse to visit. The white and black rocks are in a plastic baggie, along with the lighter I bought in Cee and the three letters. The clamshells have their own container. Ignoring my spinning head, I fasten my laces. My ankle is almost back to its pre-Camino size.

The walk to the lighthouse is steep and windy. Perhaps it's the lingering effects of vomiting all night, but it's the hardest three kilometres I've walked. Watching the sun set tonight will feel particularly saintly. But when I get there, there is no sun – only cloud.

A little concrete marker stands to attention, similar to the one on the Primitivo that I thought was telling me to smile. It says *0,00 K.M.* The end of the road. Or just the beginning.

I scan the stalls dotted all over the place. A wonderland of plastic. Fridge magnets, dream catchers, flags, little bottles filled with sand, Camino scallops. I will not look. I am a *pilgrim*, not a common tourist.

With the wind howling, I clamber over boulders. At the farthest rocky outreach, I'm overcome by dizziness. Clamshell in hand, my mind goes blank. Do the clams represent wishes or sins? Am I confessing? Or what? *Dear Lord*. All this way and I have forgotten what the point of it all is. I toss the shells into the Atlantic, hoping for the best.

All around me is scorched stone. It is here that pilgrims burn whatever they hope to leave behind. A crematorium of disappointment, heartache and loss. *Ashes to ashes*.

I pull the first letter from the baggie. It's from my father, dated a month before he died. He had mailed it to Canada, where my new husband and I were traveling. The letter had been forwarded to each new address, just missing us each time. In some kind of postal wonder, it found its way back to South Africa when I was eight-and-a-half months pregnant with my son, and my father had been dead for the same amount of time.

In meticulous detail, my father explained the various insurance policies, household expenses, pension and medical plans "in the event of anything happening." *Anything*. His letter told me what he couldn't tell me on the phone, what no-one told me, that he was dying.

My father's death left my mother, at age fifty, inconveniently alone for the first time in her life. Within weeks she purged the house of almost everything they'd accumulated over the course of their marriage. Home movies. Records. Furniture. My father's clothes. The ukulele that used to strum "When the Saints Go Marching In." The projector and slides documenting their life together. Our existence as a family-of-four. Gone. All that remained of my father, a container of ashes, was deposited in a hole in a wall in the Garden of Remembrance, not far from the Opera House.

And life went on. Because that's what it does. Marriage, motherhood and moving kept me busy. It was only years later that I remembered the sword, wondered where it was and how my life might have been different if I had it.

I don't really know why I brought my father's letter with me to Spain. He's been dead for so long. But it seemed somehow important to have him with me on this pilgrimage. Maybe to show him that I could do it. Even without his sword. The wind whips across the rocks, nearly stealing the pages from my fingers. I re-fold the letter in its familiar twenty-four-year-old creases and stow it safely in the baggie before I take out the second letter, the one from Sister Bernadette.

Crouching behind a rock, I find the lighter from Cee. The air spins furiously but I have not walked all this way to *not* burn the crap out of Sister Bernadette. On yellow stationery, a rose in one corner, Sister Bernadette's flowery writing tells me what a wonderful pupil I was. I flick the lighter expecting fireworks. An explosion of redemption. But the flame keeps dying. Of course.

The ocean is turbulent, as if some kind of battle between good and evil is being waged there. Someone sits down beside me. It takes me a moment to recognise the woman from the cathedral in Santiago de Compostela. *Venus.* Without her ponytail, her hair is as wild as the sea below. And it's longer than I imagined, reaching below her waist in ribbons of burnt umber.

"This place is magic you know." She is clearly unencumbered by superfluous social conventions such as saying hello. "The Celts used to perform their rituals here." She caresses the rock between us. "They would sit on this very rock and be given strength."

Venus tells me that the route the Camino follows is a reflection of the Milky Way above, which is why its energy is so special. "Sometimes lovers came. Women who couldn't bear children. They'd lie naked under the moonlight. Perform fantastic fertility rituals. Make love. Over and over. *Et voilà!* A baby."

Do people still do that? Come here to make babies? What a fantastic story to someday tell your children.

"And it was on a rock like this that Saint James' body landed after floating along the Coast of Death on his rudderless stone ship. It was accompanied all the way by celestial music and angels. Can you imagine that?"

I can.

She tells me about Celtic Queen Lupa, who would not give James' followers permission to bury his body here. "She sent troops after them. But a bridge collapsed and all her troops were killed. She immediately converted to Christianity and provided James' followers with a cart and an ox to find a resting place for his body."

If Lupa's story tells us anything, it's that faith, contrary to Sister Bernadette's claim, isn't a gift. It's not grace. It's what we cling to out of fear. Maybe faith is simply what we keep in our back pocket, like my mascara tucked away in Petunia, just in case.

But this is not a conversation I want to have with Venus. So I say, politely, "What a lovely name. Lupa."

"Yes," she agrees. "She-wolf."

"I wonder if she was white or black." I'm not speaking so much as thinking out loud, but Venus seems to understand my question.

"I suspect both," she says. "Isn't that the way it works?" Our thighs almost touching, I feel the heat of her legs. She pulls at the gold band on her ring finger, sliding it on and off, on and off, without looking at it. It's plain, like mine and she also doesn't wear an engagement ring. I count four whooshes as the waves cavort below us.

"I expected so much." She squeezes one eye shut and holds the ring up to the light, squinting into it as if there's an answer waiting up in the clouds for her. Another three whooshes. They sound further away. "But a road can't save you." She slips the ring back on. "Even a mystical road like this."

I should be annoyed with this woman, whose name I do not know, who has interrupted my ritual on the rocks. But she feels like a message in a bottle. A promise made long ago.

She reaches into her jacket pocket. "Here." She gives me a large scallop shell with the red cross of Saint James on it. It's the one I have refused to carry, in defiance of pilgrim convention. I don't want it. I've successfully avoided it my entire pilgrimage.

I take it. "Thank-you." Such a coward.

Venus stands. Framed by the volatile skies of the Costa da Morte, she slips off her ring again, puts it in the palm of her hand, gazes at it one last time, and then tosses it into the ocean.

"It's just a road," she says and turns, walking into the wind.

27

I return Sister Bernadette's letter to the baggie, unburned, and find the third note. From Adam. On a sheet of plain white paper, it contains only twelve words, written in blue ink. They are words I know well. *There is a crack in everything, that's how the light gets in.*

These are the words Leonard sang the day I first felt the Crazy, watching the coffee stain spread on the living room rug. Words that described my life perfectly at the time. Words that describe many lives perfectly. Because, what I have discovered, is that I am, sadly, not special after all. Not Chosen. Despite Father Ignatius' whispered promise to me that day in his office, his priestly fingers on my forehead, inflaming me with fervour. Now, more than thirty-five years later, I can see his words for what they were: simply a way to encourage the good behaviour – the virtue – of an impressionable teenager. He probably said the same thing to all the girls.

Contemplating Adam's writing – Leonard's words – I think of all the time I spent tiptoeing between the cracks. Vigilantly avoiding the darkness hiding beneath. Rigidly following rules I didn't understand. And while I have always loved Leonard, I do believe he got this wrong: the thing about cracks isn't that they let the light in, it's that they let the darkness out. And that's where the beauty is hiding.

The wind dies down and this time the yellow lighter does not falter. I send Adam back to the universe in flames, with love, whatever that's worth. Because Adam stepped into the Crazy and danced with the black wolf. Wanting nothing more than simply to dance.

The clouds shimmy away, exposing the setting sun. A beam of light reaches across the ocean towards me. I think of all the incarnations of Saint James that I have encountered along my pilgrimage. And all the versions of myself. How do I know which one is real?

Saint James on his ornate throne in the cathedral, all glitzy and showy, sinks into the Atlantic, along with Luna Blue's toolbox filled with glitter and dreams. Next, Saint James the Moor-slayer, victorious on his white stallion, gallops into the shrinking tunnel of light, taking with him my Big Life. And when the sun disappears off the Ends of the Earth, only Saint James the pilgrim, with his scallop shell and bucket hat, remains. And still there are no answers.

So many questions have accompanied me along the way. Questions about good and bad, right and wrong, love, life, death, myself. They have burrowed their way into my jiggling bones, holding me together, breaking me apart.

I don't want Venus' scallop shell. But how can I leave it behind? It contains her story. A tiny, precious piece of her truth. I close my fingers around it, as though it were the Holy Grail. I, its guardian.

The boulders surrounding me are cluttered with inukshuks that remind me of home. Vancouver. I contemplate adding my two little rocks to the stone figure nearest me, but this seems too ordinary. So I pocket them again and start back down the hill.

With the sun gone, the road is in darkness. I walk quickly, my ears ringing, as if the wind is alive in my eardrums. At the outskirts of town, I take the side street back to my linoleum-floor room with its double bed.

My dreams are filled with wild women dancing on rocks, flames leaping from their heads. One of them leans into me, whispers something I can't hear. A snake slithers from her head and wraps itself around my ankle. And I watch, as though from Heaven, as a web of fine cracks spreads across my body. And then a tremor rises from somewhere in the middle of the earth and I disintegrate. All that is left of me is a pile of ash. Yellow. Like sulphur. The colour of cowardice.

The pounding in my ankle wakes me. The dream still fresh in my head, I hold my breath and lift the sheet. No ash. No snake. Just a swollen ankle again. It must have been the icy downhill trudge last night.

It's my last day in Spain. Tomorrow I start my journey back to real life. I need to squeeze as much out of Finisterre as possible today. There's a church across the road I want to see so I grab Tom's last ice-pack and hobble towards it. Finding a sunny space on the step outside, I crack the ice and wrap it around my ankle while I wait for the church doors to open.

"Canada!" Tom and his turquoise eyes appear at the steps. He plonks himself next to me, lifts my foot and rearranges the ice-pack as if he owns it, which I suppose he does. "What would you do without me?"

"I don't know Tom. I just don't know," I say. "You're my knight in shining armour."

"Let me see this ankle." He removes my shoe, prodding my foot. Why does this feel so normal?

"Your backpack seems smaller?"

"It is," he smiles. "No more paintings."

"Paintings?"

His fingers find the sensitive spot. I barely flinch.

"Remember the painter who fucked my wife?"

I nod my head.

"There were two of his paintings in the house. Of Gloria. One in the bathroom – right next to the shower where I found them. And one in the kitchen." He presses his fingers firmly up and down my calf. Then my shin. "I was going to throw them in the trash. But this seemed so much sweeter," he laughs. "Until the Pyrenees." Tom had started his Camino in France, in the mountains. "Jesus! I hated the two of them in the Pyrenees. Do you have any idea how much those fucking paintings weighed?"

"But where are they now?" I ask.

"I burnt them at the lighthouse."

"Really?" I had trouble burning a letter. And he burnt two paintings?

"What was that like?"

"Fucking awesome." Tom slips my shoe back on and tightens the laces. "Gloria's head disappeared in a puff of smoke. I almost believed in God."

"How long did it take?"

"Maybe ten minutes. I've never seen anything burn that fast. Probably because it was crap."

I tell him about Sister Bernadette's letter. That it wouldn't burn.

"It obviously wasn't meant to be destroyed," he says.

"Now you're the expert on pilgrimages?" I laugh.

Tom is taking the bus back to Santiago de Compostela today, and then flying home to Tasmania.

"Wanna walk with me to the station in a bit?" he asks.

"Sure. But I have to go in here first." I point to the church behind us, where one door is now cracked open.

"I'll wander around out here," he says. "My last bit of fresh air for a while."

It's dark inside the chapel but my eyes adjust quickly. Conspicuously absent are the religious trappings that have cluttered so many of the churches along the Camino. No neon halos or porcelain cherubs with Shirley Temple curls. No crocheted roses or plastic baby Jesus. No Saint James, in any of his embodiments. Only a wooden cross on the wall behind the altar.

I'm standing in the aisle when "Panis Angelicus" slices the air. An organ. Where is it? I close my eyes and turn slowly, trying to pinpoint its location. It feels like the first morning of my pilgrimage, at the bottom of the walkway in Portugalete, not knowing which way to go. Twenty-one days later things are no clearer. Lifting my arms, I tilt my head and listen. To the music. To God.

The atmosphere changes. Opening my eyes, I see Tom in the doorway, more shadow than man. One hand on the door, his leg seems suspended in mid-air, undecided. The tension in his body is palpable.

I lower my arms. Tom crosses the threshold. Music fills the space between us. Halfway down the aisle he drops his backpack into a pew and bows deeply. His face is hidden in the shadows, so I don't know if he's making fun of me. Reciprocating with an awkward curtsey, I step towards him. His one hand clasps my fingers. The other rests shyly on my back. Some unseen energy closes the church door, extinguishing the light. The base of my spine flickers.

"You're in church," I whisper. Two eyes glow at us from the pew.

Tom pulls me closer, his breath jagged in my hair, his fingers trembling. And we dance. Two pilgrims. I will remember this moment forever. The music. Our hearts beating. Each in the other's chest. Tom's fingers holding mine.

"Panic Angelicus" ends. Uncertainty flutters in Tom's shoulders. With no music, he stops moving. So do I. Because that's how dancing works. It fuses you. But it is a brief pause. Tom's body sighs and then we are moving again. In sacred silence. Prayers twinkle in my feet. For family, friends, the home that is waiting for me, the strangers that have grown my soul. And for all the times that magic has been made by dancing in the dark.

Tom is facing the door when it opens. A breeze? He pulls away slightly. His eyes are luminous – two planets. I'm the one in the shadows now. The organ starts up again. "Hail Mary." I have nowhere to look but into Tom's eyes and I finally get it, more than forty years after discovering the Kama Sutra in Amy's attic. It's not the Holy Ghost those naked men and women were seeing in each other's eyes. They were seeing their Holy Selves.

It's myself I see in Tom's eyes: the ballerina waiting backstage, the teenage schoolgirl skipping past the bougainvillea, the twenty-two-year-old virgin who was going to change the world. In Tom's eyes, she exists again.

"I see you," I whisper. To her. To me. To the Me in Him and the Him in Me.

Tom says, "I see you too."

28

A stream of Spanish shatters the moment and a miniature man wearing a Santa hat rushes towards us. A Santa hat? In June? I have no clue what he's saying but Tom and I have clearly broken some kind of rule.

Tom grabs his pack. "Geez, Canada. First time in forty years I go into a church, and you get me in trouble."

We head into the sunshine, and the kitten who had been staring at us from the pew shoots past our legs.

At the station, the bus is waiting.

"Where are the rocks?" Tom asks.

I reach into my pocket and pull them out.

"Jesus! You've still got those fucking rocks! Why didn't you leave them at the lighthouse?"

"Because that's what everyone does."

"Oh, so you're *special*," he laughs. "You're not *like* everyone else."

I scowl at him, then put the rocks back in my pocket as the passengers start boarding.

"Guess I gotta go." Tom hugs me. Hard. "I'll miss you, kiddo."

I wonder if I'll ever see eyes this colour again.

Just before he disappears into the bus, he yells: "They're just fucking rocks, Canada!"

The bus leaves the station, taking Tom with it. I think of all the pilgrims I've walked with, laughed with, slept with, eaten with, got rained on with, had deep conversations with. And how everyone has disappeared back into their own lives, lives in which I have no place.

Tom's ice pack has worked splendidly. My ankle barely aches as I head for the lighthouse and my last ritual. On the steps, where Tom found me earlier, a kitten is sleeping. This must be the creature that watched us dance in the church. I sit beside him. He hops onto my legs, circles a few times, makes himself comfortable. I ignore the pilgrim warnings about Camino cats. Apparently they're riddled with disease, like ringworm and who-knows-what-else. As I stroke his mottled back, he purrs.

You can't possess a cat. Cats decide whether you're worthy of their attention. Even Charlie, who was happy to wear dolls' clothes and lie in the stroller – I understood that he was the boss. All you can do is love a cat, with no presumption that he'll love you back. But when he does, you pay attention, so that when he leaves again, which he will, you remember what it is to be loved like that. With no expectations or demands. No judgement.

Lifting the kitten, I say, "Sorry, little guy, I have to get going. It was nice meeting you." I put him back on the step and he curls up exactly where I found him and closes his eyes. I'm already forgotten.

The walk out of Finisterre today is hot and sunny, with none of yesterday's wind or fog. I pass a graveyard I did not notice yesterday. I had such high hopes for my Spanish cemetery encounters. But except for the rare gem, like

Comillas with its Avenging Angel, most of them have been disappointing. This one is no different, with its walls of crumbling bricks. Pink and white daisies trail across one ledge, mocking death. How did they spring up in the middle of this concrete block?

The rusty plaque on the top tier tells me that this is the final resting place of Domingo Fernandez. On the bottom is Carmen, his daughter. Between the two of them is a space, presumably for Domingo's wife, Carmen's mother. But a sign, held in place by a large rock, says *Se Vende*. For sale. The phone number, in black marker, is starting to fade. Why is it for sale? What did Domingo's wife do to be excluded from eternal rest with her family? Did she abandon them? Or did they banish her? Did she have an affair? Commit murder? How irredeemable *was* her sin?

I consider the question the stranger with the Costco handkerchief asked me in East Vancouver: what is enough? Love means such different things to different people. And I suddenly understand the magnificence of Sarah's epitaph: *Wife and Mother*. What a privilege it is.

I touch the empty space between Domingo and Carmen. Is Victoria-the-medium right? Am I the only one judging myself? The man in the black hat?

A faded beetle, on his back in the daisies, kicks his spiky legs frantically in the air. I remember learning, in grade 5, that in ancient Egypt, Scarab beetles were buried with the mummified bodies of the newly dead. For weeks I worried about those beetles. Did someone leave them food? How long did it take for them to die? Did they know they would never see sunlight again?

The beetle on the Fernandez bricks stares at me from his upside-downness. He isn't pretty, kind of like a dung beetle. Does he understand that if no one turns him over, he will die? A little nudge from my pinkie finger tips him right side up again. And just like that he lives another day. I am the Messiah.

He buzzes away, no sign of gratitude, as a rooster waddles towards me. Three friends join him, their webbed feet so brightly yellow they seem freshly pedicured. They flip their shiny tail feathers as they strut about, circling me. Camino drag queens. Unlike the cow in Portugalete, there is no judgement in their orange eyes as they examine me. Only curiosity. As if they understand that life is an ever-changing plethora of possibilities. And that we ought to grab as many of them as we can. Because they will not last forever.

Corn on the side of the road is all it takes for the roosters to lose interest in me. They swagger off to eat and I keep going. The book at the Ends of the Earth is waiting. This is where pilgrims write their names, along with whatever wisdom they have gathered along the Way. I have no idea what I will write. I have collected nothing but seashells. And more questions. God has given me no answers. Are my questions so unholy? So unworthy of his time?

On the outskirts of town, I see her. Standing in the doorway of an old stone house, a bride is swaying in time to music that is drifting out into the street. A waltz. *One, two, three. Two, two, three.* Her dress is uncluttered, a sprig of flowers in her hair. She is beautiful. And happy. *Three, two, three.* An older man joins her. Her father. He kisses her on both cheeks. Then he takes her arm in his, the way my father did almost a quarter century ago.

This young woman, a girl really, has no idea what the rest of her life will be like. And yet, here she stands, ready to take a chance on another human being. On herself. Perhaps committing to love *is* the greatest kind of bravery there is.

I want to tell her to find a dance that only she and her beloved can do. *And dance it every day. Together,* I want to say. *With awe. Because if you don't, twenty years from now there will be between the two of you only four left feet. You will blame him. Of course. But it's not his fault you lost yourself. And then, sweet bride, you will have to decide: when you set out to find your soul again — your Self — do you do it alone? Or with him by your side?*

But all I say, as she passes me, is "Guapa."

"Gracias," she smiles, and walks towards the church, arm-in-arm with her father. She doesn't even glance down, doesn't care about cracks.

At the lighthouse, I find the big book, with almost the same dimensions as the Kama Sutra in Amy's attic. I hold my white and black rocks, one in each palm, feeling their heaviness. I've been hanging on to them in the same way that I've been clinging to the stories I've been telling myself about my childhood, my family, my marriage. *They don't mean anything, Canada. They're just fucking rocks.* But what does *anything* mean, then?

Maybe the woman with the scythe was my messenger after all. And perhaps what I saw in her eyes was simply that there is no Big Life for me. I have saved no-one. I probably never will.

From my back pocket I pull Venus' scallop shell. The one I did not want. It reminds me now of the one my son gave me at Ambleside Beach, when all I could promise my children was magic. And it has given me the words I've been seeking. I lay the rocks next to the book, little refugees, and I write.

Lindy-Lou. She collects seashells and unholy questions.
Nothing more.
A little life.
But it is mine.
Guapa.

POSTLUDE

West Vancouver

It's been two years since I walked the Way of Saint James. And every night, my last words before falling asleep are *thank-you*. The same thing I engraved on the candle in Cee. For my family. My home. Love. Even the goddamn fence.

Venus was right. The Camino is just a road. It holds no answers, no divine potions hidden under mystical rocks. God is no more to be found in the gravel on a pilgrimage in northern Spain than he is in the asphalt in West Vancouver on the way to Starbucks.

Maybe my questions remain unanswered simply to remind me that possibility exists. Dancing in the dark. Watching my children breathe. Finding myself in strangers' eyes. Not knowing what will happen next. Maybe the point – the beauty of it – is simply to keep asking.

There are still days when I feel the missingness. The unlived life remains alluring precisely because it's not real. Because it exists only in its most perfect version. And when I feel the stirring in my spine, whispering, *if you just had more courage*, I remind myself that the line separating courage and recklessness is flimsy. Like the fragile tendrils between sanity and lunacy. Life and death. Shadow and light.

Then I put on my hiking shoes, purple now, and move my feet, like the African proverb. Some days I walk in silence, but mostly there is music in my head. And sometimes, I confess, my tie dye leggings strut. The Crazy sparkles. I hold on.

It's my father's birthday today. He should have been eighty-two. Not dead. I dial my mother's number. She in South Africa, in the city with the Opera House. Me on my deck in Eagle Harbour, the first white flowers opening on the magnolia tree. How does this happen every year? Despite my inattention?

"Hello, Ma."

A hummingbird hovers above the wildflowers in the terracotta pot. It's the same pot, but the flowers are new.

"What's the matter?" she says.

"What did you do with Pa's sword?"

The hummingbird's wings move so quickly that they seem not to be moving at all. He appears to be simply hanging in the air, immune to gravity, a tiny unidentified flying object.

"Ma?" I want to hear her apologise. For throwing away my destiny.

The little bird's beak disappears into a pink trumpet-like flower whose name I don't know.

After a very long silence, my mother says, "It's under my bed."

I can't breathe. *Mother of God.* My father's sword has been under her bed all this time?

"You can have it if you want," she adds.

The hummingbird disappears. And I see, for the first time, the crack running the length of the pot. Granules of soil peek through the clay fracture – darkness breaking free. I huddle beside the pot, just as I did after writing my birthday letter to my husband, two-and-a-half years ago. I run my palm above the crack, carefully avoiding it.

Then I inhale deeply and push my finger into the jaggedness. Like a sword. My father's sword. *My* sword. Not lost after all, but patiently waiting for me.

The pot splits in two, spewing its pitch black dirt all over me.

What now?

Acknowledgements

Thank-you to everyone who helped bring this little book into the world. Your support and encouragement have made my heart so full. Enormous gratitude to all who read any of the *many* drafts, specially Tammy, Susan, Elana, Jennifer, Susanne and Vicky. Your insights and suggestions, delivered so kindly, kept me going.

A humongous thanks to my family for giving me so much to write about. To my mother, my husband and my children – big hugs for your patience and for keeping the eye-rolling mostly behind my back. To my sister, Megan, who reminded me that memory is a fickle thing, and that mine is particularly selective. And who said I could write it anyway. I love you. You see, I said it out loud.

And to the remarkable adolescents whose questions, written by hand on cue cards, and in my heart during our circles, accompanied me on my pilgrimage: I can't wait to see how you transform our world. Keep asking questions. Specially the unholy ones. The ones with no answers. Because they are the most beautiful.

Writing is only half the process. Being heard is where the magic happens. So thank-you for reading my words. I would love to hear your thoughts. Please consider leaving a review on Amazon. Or a question. It would make me so very happy.

xoxo Lindy

Made in the USA
San Bernardino, CA
22 January 2020